FROM DESIRE TO DESTINY: SEVEN KEYS TO YOUR MARKETPLACE MINISTRY

JOHN S. GARFIELD

RELEASING KINGS PUBLISHING

KENNEWICK, WASHINGTON

© 2007 by John S. Garfield
First Printing, July, 2007

Releasing Kings Publishing
2736 Kyle Rd
Kennewick, WA 99338 USA
509-248-5837, 509-308-6873
e-mail: office@worldcastpublishing.com
Web Sites: www.worldcastpublishing.com
            www.Releasing-Kings.com

ISBN 13: 978-0-615-14767-3
Cover by Paul Jones

REVIEWS

John—First let me take a moment to say how wonderful I think the new book is. What a grace God has given you to be able to express the marketplace ministry in such a clear format. After reading your book I was re-inspired by God's concept of reaching the world through our heart's desires. I encourage you to read and re-read each chapter allowing the Holy Spirit to draw a map and point you in a new direction. The Marketplace is truly where the breath of God is blowing. I encourage you to join in the fun and see God touch lives.

Dawnya Sasse, www.teaevents.com

When I first met John, I could tell instantly what ignites his heart and passion. *Desire to Destiny* spells it out clearly and profoundly. John provides both a theological and practical framework for understanding the potential of those in the marketplace. Barriers between work and faith—business and missions—are melting and God is using an unexpected platform to transform individuals, businesses, and nations. Imagine the impact we could have on this world by just capturing and living our dreams. This book is a must read for businesspeople as well as pastors and church leaders who desire to know more about those who make up their congregations.

Mark Charles, www.a-crossborders.org

John Garfield's book, *Desire to Destiny: Seven Keys to Your Marketplace Ministry,* helps equip and inspire Christian business people to change their world. As one who works with both ministry leaders and business leaders in North America and overseas, I pray this work brings another level of partnership between the business leader and their pastor. Together, kings and priests will impact our cities, our government, and our destiny.

Mel C. Mullen, Word of Life Centre,
Red Deer, Alberta, www.wordoflife.ca

Desire to Destiny stirred the depths of my heart. I was challenged to follow my God-given desires as I serve Him in my marketplace. My vision was expanded, my passion for representing Him was ignited, and my life was challenged to be more balanced as I follow Him more closely. I found this book to be simple, yet biblical to the core. It certainly stretched my thinking. The practical steps and exercises were very helpful. I was encouraged that His Kingdom is within us, and we are to represent Him in our workplace. John presents a balanced view of God's sovereignty and our part in His plan.

Kent Humphreys, President
Fellowship of Companies for Christ, www.fcci.org

Desire to Destiny confronts a good idea run amok. For too long the over emphasis on "waiting for God" has left many in the Body of Christ with the unbiblical belief that *waiting* is all we can do or are supposed to do as we stand still in anticipation that destiny will occur whether we do anything or not. John reminds us that we are to be co-laborers with God in transforming the kingdom that "is" into the kingdom "come." To deny the responsibility God has entrusted to humanity in the management of the earth is to have a diminished view as to what the life of Jesus was about.

Linda Rios Brook, President
Rios Brook Foundation, www.riosbrook.org

John's new book *Desire to Destiny,* has capsulated a progressive vision for marketplace ministry that is prime for the hour. The book communicates a business-ministry model that is easy to understand and attainable for anyone with a little initiative. I greatly appreciate the bottom line focus on wealth for a purpose, reaching the world for Christ. This book is far superior to your first book in content and instilling practical vision. Well done John!

Duane Smith, Investment Specialist—Realtor®
www.tricitiesconnection.com

It is clear that John Garfield has his finger on the pulse of God's direction for the Kingdom. He is a pioneer among church leaders who are taking a fresh look at this incredible move of God in the marketplace. *From Desire to Destiny: Seven Keys To Your Marketplace Ministry* is a clarion call for the Body of Christ to bridge the gap between business and work and to partner together as God intended. This awesome book is that tool to equip Kings and Priests to realize that we are all on the winning team, i.e., God's team. This relevant message is for this hour.

Pat Moore, Director/Marketplace Minister,
Center for Business Excellence

A prophet spoke over me years ago, that the move of God that I was born for was not yet in the earth. I wondered as I wandered, I struggled with walking away from a ministry that was somewhat fulfilling but just not me. My destiny was not being lived out, and I knew it.

Releasing Kings was like a breath of fresh air; confirmation and the final dose of permission that I needed to march ahead whole heartedly. Living this message is amazing. It often scares me, like Peter ready to step out of the boat into the unknown. But my destiny is being pursued, and it is rewarding.

John Garfield has taken the next step, the practical step. *Desire to Destiny* is the nuts and bolts of the message. Clearly the time has come. The move of God is in the earth. God's people are receiving the authority to live the message, the freedom to be the expression of God in the earth, and the confidence to know and understand that their life is ministry. Our eyes have been opened. *Desire to Destiny* gives the practical insight and guidance to take the next step.

John Laney, Project Manger, Developer
www.fluidynamics.com

Just as professionals in every area of the marketplace keep copies of books, manuals, and text for quick reference during their working hours, John's book should be treated as such for the serious Kingdom-minded person. During consultations with International Christian Business Leaders over the past 12 months, I have heard on several occasions that they struggled with what seems to be a fragmentation. I believe *Desire to Destiny* is designed to equip you, in such a way, as to be positioned to bring strength and unity to the Body of Christ. My prayer is that as you study John's book you would receive clarity of the solutions that exist to the challenges before you. I thank you John, for your obvious perseverance.

Robert Kinsella—President & CEO,
Alberta, Canada, www.placeofwealth.com

John Garfield has written a magnificent follow up to *Releasing Kings,* with his new book, *Desire to Destiny.* It is a wonderful testimony and primer for all those who have even the smallest feeling there is more. There is! John reminds us, in the plain words of those of us in the marketplace every day, what a father does and how to recognize we live in the Kingdom now if we will truly believe and live in a full relationship with God.

The book mirrors so much of my wife and my walk with the Lord these past seven years, that it is exciting to find there are indeed many others on the same path. The power of networking and sharing our testimonies cannot be emphasized enough. If indeed "we overcome by the power of the blood and the word our testimony," then we must learn to express it and live it for others to see, not just hear. John's new book is a tremendous reminder and aid for us engaged in it and for all who desire to follow. I highly recommend it.

Bruce P. Gerhart, Midwest Regional Manager,
Love Funding Corporation, www.lovefunding.com

I recently had the opportunity of working with John Garfield during our first *Releasing Kings* Conference in Alberta, Canada. It's one thing reading his books, which I know can personally ignite a divine "spark" in the entrepreneur's heart. It's another thing to work with John in the marketplace. Susan and I are privileged to be partnering with John on "Releasing Kings" Conferences, and helping with some of the mentoring services and new website for *Desire to Destiny,* www.desiretodestiny.com. As a couple, Susan and I continue to be impacted and our own dreams being fulfilled. *Desire to Destiny* will give you practical steps and tools to implement that "freedom" received from *Releasing Kings. Desire to Destiny* will help you take bold decisive steps expressing your gifts and talents to those who need them most. God's anointing is all over this message! God gets excited about people that boldly express the freedom they've received, and spread this throughout the marketplace. John's heart is to help do for you what he is doing for us. So trust your heart, believe that "passion" that makes you come alive, and boldly take the steps to a great adventure. We would be overjoyed to hear your story.

David and Susan Harris,
Airdrie, Alberta, www.desiretodestiny.com

FROM DESIRE TO DESTINY:
SEVEN KEYS TO YOUR MARKETPLACE MINISTRY

FOREWARD

I t is time for God's people to be the head rather than the tail. The presence of righteousness is needed in every area of society including business, government, education, communication, sales, and services. God is calling people to rise out of mediocrity, accept responsibility, and take positions of leadership.

Relating to these subjects, I had the privilege of co-authoring an earlier book with John Garfield entitled, *Releasing Kings for Ministry in the Marketplace*. We have had a terrific response with communications from all over the world. Individuals, Bible study groups, and churches have embraced the message of kings in the marketplace. As a result, dedicated Christians have gone out full of faith and more confidence to impact the world for the Kingdom of God.

Now John has developed this message even further, with a passion to inspire Christians to respond to the call of God in all areas of society. John is creating faith and excitement in those who are willing to succeed. He is removing obstacles which exist in the minds of the hesitant. He is provoking those who sit in the starting gates. He is injecting fire in the hearts of those who are willing, and he is releasing the entrepreneurial spirit. John is challenging God's people to walk the streets where Jesus would walk—the streets of the business world and community right around you.

Meditate on the words written herein and you will see yourself being propelled forward.

Harold R. Eberle
President of Worldcast Ministries and Publishing

You will be blessed in the city and blessed in the country.

The fruit of your womb will be blessed, and the crops of your land and the young of your livestock—the calves of your herds and the lambs of your flocks.

Your basket and your kneading trough will be blessed.

You will be blessed when you come in and blessed when you go out.

The LORD will grant that the enemies who rise up against you will be defeated before you. They will come at you from one direction but flee from you in seven.

The LORD will send a blessing on your barns and on everything you put your hand to. The LORD your God will bless you in the land he is giving you.

The LORD will establish you as his holy people, as he promised you on oath, if you keep the commands of the LORD your God and walk in his ways. Then all the peoples on earth will see that you are called by the name of the LORD, and they will fear you. The LORD will grant you abundant prosperity—in the fruit of your womb, the young of your livestock and the crops of your ground—in the land he swore to your forefathers to give you.

The LORD will open the heavens, the storehouse of his bounty, to send rain on your land in season and to bless all the work of your hands. You will lend to many nations but will borrow from none. The LORD will make you the head, not the tail. If you pay attention to the commands of the LORD your God that I give you this day and carefully follow them, you will always be at the top, never at the bottom. Do not turn aside from any of the commands I give you today, to the right or to the left, following other gods and serving them. (Deuteronomy 28:3–14)

PREFACE

The Father's heart is delighted in this hour to see the saints doing the work of the ministry. Creation is eagerly waiting the day when these sons will be revealed in all their glory (Romans 8:18–19). The "day" is today and the marketplace is the forum for ministry. The first fruits are an entrepreneurial, conquering, creative, and contagious generation of men and women being released into prosperity and ministry right now. We used "Kings" to describe this exciting and growing dynamic among God's people.

Implementing the desires in millions of individual hearts to express the destiny God has in mind for the earth is both global and personal. The marriage of personal dreams with God's purpose launches an adventure more exciting and fulfilling than we ever imagined. The revelation to connect our personal life (vocation, business, hobbies, gifts, interests, passions, etc.) with God's plan to take the gospel to the ends of the earth and bless the nations is the journey of a lifetime. The greatest trademark of a Kingly lifestyle is that it's *fun*. Helping people connect with their own hearts and experience their own success in measurable increments of creativity, prosperity, and ministry is simply a thrill and a privilege. Servants are being graduated to "friend" status with Jesus and the ramifications go far beyond punching the clock until retirement.

Special thanks to Harold Eberle for laying a foundation in theology for marketplace ministry. We listed his "must reads" in Appendix A. David Harris provided the thought questions and exercises at the end of each section. He's leading the charge to implement a coaching ingredient to the message of this book through www.desiretodestiny.com. Annette Bradley provided the final edit and managed the publication. Lee Pierce put the book in the final layout and incorporated a million comments. Paul Jones created the cover. Thanks for your patience and help.

God has given by some great examples of Kings that already exemplify the message in this book. At some level God has mysteriously and wonderfully knit our hearts together for this common cause of releasing more Kings. God adds more all the time so the list is incomplete, but I want to personally thank those that have been an encouragement and example to me: John Laney, Del Olivarez, Duane Smith, Howard Ferris, Dawnya Sasse, Andy Briesmeister, Mark Charles, Mike Nelson, Don Ward, and David Harris. Most have a story of their Kingly exploits on our interview page.

I often get a surprising response from Kings exposed to this message for the first time. It goes something like this: "Please take me with you. I want to be part of what you're doing." I feel the same way and I've purposed in my heart to take an army to a new level. You see, we're all anxious in our hearts to do what the Father is doing and be about His business. It really is a reformation.

INTRODUCTION

*R*eleasing Kings for Ministry in the Marketplace (our first book) is a great foundation for marketplace ministry, from its biblical roots to its outworking in our lives. Since its publication in 2004, it has resonated with people around the world. The sequel is obviously, "How do I get started?" Becoming more Kingly, entrepreneurial, and missions-minded in the Kingdom is a transition that implements some of the new wings in our theological house . . . breaking poverty for example. To help the legion of spiritual entrepreneurs take their places in the Kingdom, we've created seven simple steps that can be a roadmap to your personal adventure.

1. I'm Prophetic—God and I Talk
    a. What has God written on my heart?
    b. What's He doing in the Kingdom?
2. I'm Passionate—Following the Desires of My Heart
    a. Allowing myself to experience the emotions of a dream-come-true.
    b. Building a vision to facilitate receiving my heart's desire
    c. Setting timely goals to take steps toward the vision
3. I'm Purposeful—Bridging My Desires and God's Plan
    a. Feeling God's specific permission to pursue my passion
    b. Connecting the dots between God's will for my life and my passion, history, talents, personality, etc.
4. I Have a Plan for Product(s)—Adding Value to the Lives of Others (Ministry)

   a. Packaging your passion in a way that will bless others

   b. Receiving a financial return for the value of your product

   c. Goals—the wellspring of creativity

5. I'm Moving from Profits to Prosperity—Learning to Multiply

   a. Learning to multiply your profit into wealth

   b. Learn to multiply your own efforts with disciples, employees, and networking

6. I have a Mission—Blessing the Nations

   a. Leveraging your ministry/business to bless the nations

   b. Providing an incentive for your disciples or staff to take your business/ministry elsewhere

7. I'm Contagious—Viral Missions

   a. Catching the next wave of a grass roots movement

   b. Missions done God's way is fun, contagious, and it carries the ingredient of prosperity

KEY I
I'M PROPHETIC—GOD AND I TALK

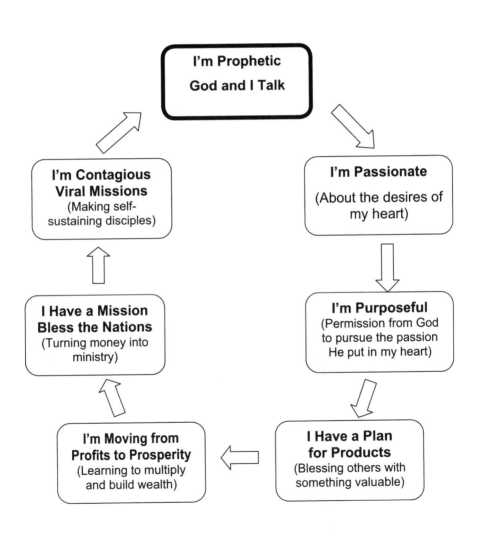

W riting a "one-size-fits-all" recipe to launch your life might seem as if we are trying to eat an elephant in one sitting. However, we have learned that there are some bite-sized pieces that we can offer; a progression toward your life's purpose that can be embraced with some hope of getting there. It starts with God. When we understand how He operates and relates to us, the fog starts to lift and the essentials come into view.

Introspection—Self examination is all that secular life coaches have to offer! God really does grant the desires of our hearts. Our hearts naturally gravitate toward what He's doing in the earth. If you want to know what really will put passion in your own heart, you'll want to take a peek at what God is doing. It's pretty exciting!

Sovereignty—God has a plan but He leaves it "open" for you to participate. "Sovereignty" means He has the power to do anything He wants (and occasionally does), but He usually works through people as a first preference. That promotes initiative to a place of importance in our walk with God. We play a big role in choosing our destiny.

Guidance—When we mature from "servant" to "friend," God starts asking us to make many of the decisions. That's the point where some Christians will fail, while Kings excel. When we finally understand that God is asking us what role we want to play, the guilt over being independent and rebellious stops, and the adventure in co-laboring begins.

Kingdom When? Kings who are willing to make decisions discover that the job of expanding the Kingdom isn't reserved for the millennium—it's our job right now. We can ask for the power, the finances, and the open doors to fix a broken world . . . and we should.

Good News—The good news of the Gospel isn't just about sin and the solution Jesus provided on the cross. It's about His resurrection and how to receive and live in abundant life.

"It Looks this Way." When we get our theology right and understand Who God really is, we gravitate naturally toward our heart's passion, purpose, plans, prosperity, and mission.

CHAPTER 1
INTROSPECTION—
THE SECOND FASTEST WAY TO
FIND YOUR PASSION

After class, a really nice lady was convinced for the first time that God was interested in granting her the desires of her heart. She was a little frustrated, however because she really didn't have a passion to which she could point. I suggested she read *Releasing Kings.* It dawned on me that there is quite a large group who are mature enough *not* to ask God for the wrong things. Most of us have enough dead works under our belts that we've gotten the cure (don't consume prayer on our carnal appetites). However, many Christians do not have a clear grasp on the specifics of their destinies. So, here are a few thoughts on how you can find the passion that will motivate your vocation and your ministry, and land you on your destiny.

"What's my passion?" This is a great place to start. You're already farther than you think. Many believers live their entire lives according to religious principles that never really touch their hearts. It's no fun. Coaching from a host of self-help gurus is also popular in the business world right now—it's called success coaching. It's mostly great stuff and it borrows heavily from biblical principles. However, it's still rooted in self-motivation. It works (from the head) but Christians have something that works better (from the heart), and some power to go with it—the Holy Spirit!

Finding the passion or the desire of your heart that also is rooted in God's heart is the real home run. God promises to do it—but, as with all redemptive promises, we play a role in cooperating with Him to receive the deposit in our hearts. Listen to the covenant.

> *"This is the covenant I will make with the house of Israel after that time," declares the Lord. "I will put my*

*laws in their minds and **write them on their hearts.**
I will be their God, and they will be my people. No
longer will a man teach his neighbor, or a man his
brother, saying, Know the Lord, because **they will all
know Me, from the least of them to the greatest.***"
(Hebrews 8:10–11; see also Hebrews 10:16
and Jeremiah 31:33–34) [Emp. added]

Introspection is the second-fastest way to find your heart's desire. The fastest way is getting to know Jesus at the next level. There
are four "ask whatever" promises in John that I like to quote. Each
contains a key to finding the desire of your heart, so you can ask out
of your own passion.

1. What's the Father Doing? The most fun you can have on this
planet is to catch the wind of the Holy Spirit and do what the
Father is doing. For example, I didn't invent *Releasing Kings*. It's
something that God is doing throughout the earth. It's become the
passion of my heart and the resulting conferences are a total hoot.
God has something equally exciting for all of us.

*I tell you the truth, anyone who has faith in me will
do what I have been doing. He will do even greater
things than these, because I am going to the Father.
And I will do whatever you ask in my name, so that
the Son may bring glory to the Father. You may **ask
me for anything** in my name, and I will do it.*
(John 14:12–14) [Emp. added]

Here's how it works: I'm having fun and if I run short of anything inside the desires of my heart, I just ask for it. It's God's nature
to overflow our cups . . . and you can ask whatever!

2. Hang Around God. Spend time in prayer simply talking to God.
Allow the Holy Spirit to quicken Scriptures to you as you read. When
you get an idea, meditate on it and let your dream unfold into a plan
you can work. Realize that you're important to God and His heart
longs to spend time with your heart. That's when the transfer takes

place and the creativity begins . . . and you can ask whatever!

> *If you **remain in me** and my words remain in you, **ask whatever** you wish, and it will be given you. This is to my Father's glory, that you bear much fruit, showing yourselves to be my disciples.*
> (John 15:7–8) [Emp. added]

3. Friends Know—Jesus promised to let us in on everything. When you get to see heaven's storehouse and the smorgasbord of possibilities, your heart naturally will gravitate toward a passion that aligns your history, talents, vocation, and gifts in a seamless purpose that gives your life "mission" . . . and you can ask whatever!

> *I no longer call you servants, because a servant does not know his master's business. Instead, **I have called you friends**, for everything that I learned from my Father **I have made known to you**. You did not choose me, but I chose you and appointed you to go and bear fruit—fruit that will last. Then the Father will give you **whatever you ask** in my name.*
> (John 15:15–16) [Emp. added]

4. Complete Joy. When you tap your true passion and experience the wind of God in your sails; it's pure joy. Nothing describes the exhilaration of co-laboring with God to create something new or do the impossible. Yet, that's exactly what is waiting for you and me. . . . and you can ask whatever!

> *. . . **no one will take away your joy**. In that day you will no longer ask me anything. I tell you the truth, my Father will give you whatever you ask in my name. Until now you have not asked for **anything** in my name. **Ask and you will receive**, and your joy will be complete.*
> (John 16:22–24) [Emp. added]

Every few days my heart leaps, and I give it permission to jump and shout "Yippee!"

Homework—Make a list of the top three things that keep you from your heart's desire. Now lay that list at the foot of the cross in prayer. You even could ask the Lord to help overcome doubt.

> *"If you can?" said Jesus. "Everything is possible for him who believes." Immediately the boy's father exclaimed, "I do believe; help me overcome my unbelief!"*
> (Mark 9:23–24)

For each item on the list make a second list of ten ways you can overcome each obstacle. Ask the Lord if He has any better ideas to add to the list. Then ask Him for the power to implement the best ideas that take you into your passion . . . whatever they are. You can change the perception that "you can't" by changing your expectations for the future. Hope and faith are fleshed out with a practical plan and some goals.

Our heart naturally gravitates toward what He's doing in the earth. The result is that when we and God get on the same page, we can "ask whatever." We see it's possible by reading the verses. We understand that when we get to know a little more about the way God thinks. Christians usually box God into a version of sovereignty that requires Him to lay out every detail of the future. He's much more personable and interactive than a universal life force that can be manipulated with our thoughts and meditations. In fact, let's deal with the concept of sovereignty in the next chapter. Does He or does He not control our future?

CHAPTER 2
UNDERSTANDING THE
SOVEREIGNTY OF GOD

Accidents are a real part of life, even for Kings. Setbacks and misfortune are authentic parts of everyone's life. Often when something goes wrong, we reel in our initiative and question both our own walk and God Himself. Because Kings live so close to real life and spiritual warfare, they must have a theologically correct stance on problems—or they risk losing their willingness to be entrepreneurial, bold, and decisive.

Historic Roots—Our evangelical beliefs have surprising roots in Church fathers, such as Augustine, and in the Protestant reformation. In the fourth and fifth centuries, Christianity was subjected to Greek and Roman thought. The Middle Ages was a transition when Christian thought adopted some of the tenets of Greek philosophy. God was thought to be a prime mover or force, rather than a being having a personality and emotions. This philosophic Force was an element of the Protestant reformation when the term "sovereign" came into common use. "Sovereign" came to mean that God is the One who causes all things. In other words, He is the sole originator of all thought, decisions, and actions. This word was superimposed over the Greek-originated concept of God as a force and has come down to us essentially unchanged. There are other parallels in the stormy marriage of science and the popular theology of God's nature as shown in the table below.

When accidents happen—Because of our evangelical heritage, we're prone to think of God as being responsible. If a family loses a child, we often hear Christians consoling one another with the concept that God took the child home. This is an attempt to soften

Science	Concept of God
Aristotle & Greek Philosophy	God is the "Prime Mover" • An impersonal force, not a person
Newtonian Physics	Determinism / fatalism • Sovereignty / predestination • Prescribed future = robotic faith • Sinful nature of man
Darwin's Natural Selection	God is not the creator • Man has no soul, meaning, nor destiny • No purpose
Relativity in Physics	Relativity in morals
Quantum Physics String Theory	Chaos, nothing is predictable or knowable • Wave or particle? • Life is not real • Everything is in our imagination
Integration of Science and Spirituality	Open view of God (not a Force) • Relational, personal, conversational • Man is created in God's image • His law is in our hearts • Ruling, reigning, and creating with Him • The future is partially open, "reserved" for our participation

the blow by the belief that the child's death was known and planned by a sovereign God. According to the theology to which most of us subscribe, what happens if we assign God responsibility for the bad things that occur? In an effort to avoid resenting God and becoming bitter or rebellious, we accept whatever comes our way as God's best plan for us. We view ourselves as sinful, small, and occasionally disposable. Passivity pervades every facet of our lives. Worse yet, we move toward viewing God as impersonal, uncaring, and unreliable. We view ourselves as ants under the cosmic Lordship of a God who we neither understand nor trust. Furthermore, we never admit to ourselves or anyone else that this is true because we know it disrespects God. Wrong theology leads us to emphasize the nobility of suffering and death, rather than the life of the power of the resurrection. We naturally gravitate toward pessimism, cynicism, skepticism, doubt, unbelief, caution, wariness, and a steadfast refusal to take a risk. We must trust God in a step of faith to do something beyond our natural strength.

If, indeed, God orchestrates every detail of our lives, then logically the only thing we can do is align with our predetermined path. Under this view of God, we must be concerned primarily with avoiding rebellion, presumption, and personal ambition—all things that compete with the will of "The Force." Our spiritual disciplines are directed at zeroing out personal initiative so we don't get out of God's will. As with robots, if God doesn't touch the joy stick, we don't make a move. We're left theologically unwilling to take a risk and follow a leading that we might confuse with personal initiative or rebellious ambition. As we mature into the image of this "God" we become impersonal, uncaring, and hardened by the deaths we see in the normal course of life. Age increases our cynicism, rather than our love and enthusiasm for walking with God.

Where's Reality? God is entirely personal, emotional, and knowable. He *does not* orchestrate every detail of our future. He leaves much to our initiative, and He delights in leaving room for human enterprise. He does have a plan to redeem the world, and He does have the power to intervene whenever He chooses. However, our future is open . . . not orchestrated. Accidents can happen and God is not responsible. For example, 18 died in one accident recorded in scripture:

> *Or those eighteen who died when the tower in Siloam fell on them—do you think they were more guilty than all the others living in Jerusalem? I tell you, no!*
> (Luke 13:4–5)

After a shipwreck where the crew survived, Paul was "snakebit" . . . bad situation that was not part of God's plan and probably required some level of healing!

When the islanders saw the snake hanging from his hand, they said to each other, "This man must be a murderer; for though he escaped from the sea, justice has not allowed him to live." But Paul shook the snake off into the fire and suffered no ill effects. The people expected him to swell up or suddenly fall dead, but after waiting a long time and seeing nothing unusual happen to him, they changed their minds and said he was a god. (Acts 28:4–6)

Note that the locals ascribed to God the responsibility for his death. When that didn't happen, they decided Paul wasn't human. It was an accident that they had no theology to support!

Snake-bit? Have you suffered a loss, a failure, a setback? Of course! We all have. Did God plan to destroy a part of your life? No, He did not. Was He judging your desperately wicked, sinful heart? No, He created you and loves you unconditionally.

Mighty men who "overcome"—You see, God comes in on the resurrection side of the equation to add "life" and "blessing" to us. Once we understand who God is and really discover His nature, we can know both Him and His power. We are not insulated from accidents or suffering. We just know that when death occurs, it's a signal to start looking for the resurrection. We know a loving God who assigns angels to watch over us and protect us. We know the armor of His protection in spiritual warfare. And most of all, we know the joy that comes to the heart of our heavenly Father when we "initiate" and "create" and "exercise faith" to do the greater works that go beyond our strength and utilize His power.

Walk toward the desires of your heart. You will find God waiting for you there. Your life is a great adventure and you are scripted to be its hero. In fact, Jesus is handing you the pen to help write the script . . . and He's giving you an anointing to make it so.

Jesus said to her, "I am the resurrection and the life. He who believes in me will live, even though he dies;

and whoever lives and believes in me will never die.
Do you believe this?"   (John 11:25–26)

I believe this topic is pivotal for Kings and I'm personally drawn to knowing the actual God of the Bible, instead of the God of tradition. Here are two resources that will take you further down this path of freedom and will bless your heart:

Who is God (Chapters 17–18) by Harold Eberle

Releasing Kings (Chapters 7–8, especially page 56)

We understand that the future is not all totally determined, and that God relates to us on a personal, interactive basis. He's more than a cosmic life force that we can manipulate. Guess what? We have to revisit the whole concept of how we receive guidance. How do we balance obedience and initiative in our relationship with Jesus? That's the topic of the next chapter.

CHAPTER 3
GUIDANCE—
OBEDIENCE VS. INITIATIVE

Guidance—It is always interesting to get a read on a cross section of God's people. One question was asked over lunch after a recent conference, and it gave me a special insight into what was happening in individual lives. This is it:

*"**God led us to do** _____ in our business that had a great profit potential. But, since we took the action, we haven't seen any results. What's wrong?"*

Answer—Maybe nothing, but the phrase in bold is suspect. Our Christian culture places a huge premium on "servants" who are good at hearing and obeying God . . . as well it should. I have seldom given or heard a sermon that didn't allude to God having spoken or given some kind of direction via the Holy Spirit. Now, if God gives some kind of revelation and you're a half bubble off, it usually doesn't harm anyone. We usually have a friend who cares enough to tweak us back to the middle of the road. However, if we're a King and our decisions cost us money, that's a little different story. Being corrected after the fact doesn't restore the financial impact.

We've all been there. Most of us have felt led by God at some time to do things that didn't work. Here's the emotion with which we have to deal. "God, why did you lead me out on this limb and saw it off?" "Well, to perfect our character, of course" is the answer we gamely give ourselves. Sometimes we get so used to thinking we're being perfected in the wilderness (while everything goes wrong) that it's hard to salvage a praise report. Surprisingly, faithful believers trudge on after elevating the wonderful blessing of tribulation, trials, trouble, and loss. We simply shift our theology to the importance of suffering and prepare for the next bloody nose instead of fixing the problem.

Will real maturity please stand up? All our sermonic input has led us to believe the Holy Spirit is supposed to lead us on a daily basis. I want to suggest reverently that's patently false! All mature Christians go through fairly long stretches without hearing from God—at least on the business decision of interest. Here's the failure point of the decade—we're not supposed to be servants who just hear and obey.

> *I no longer call you servants, because a servant does not know his master's business. Instead, **I have called you friends**, for everything that I learned from my Father I have made known to you. You did not choose me, but I chose you and appointed you to go and bear fruit—fruit that will last. Then **the Father will give you whatever you ask in my name.***
>
> (John 15:14–16) [Emp. Added]

Friends—We do start our faith as servants who learn to obey . . . or we reap the consequences of God's loving discipline. However, as we mature, God elevates us to "friend" status and starts to treat us differently. He still speaks to us, but He stops making our decisions. The Holy Spirit comes alongside as our counselor, but He doesn't make our decisions for us. God doesn't have the future all pre-scripted so that we just have to get a glimpse of the cosmic monitor in prayer and act it out. The future is open regarding most of the details of our business, and God is inviting us to choose some of our own destiny. He's showing us the general plan, and then He's saying, "I'll give you whatever you ask in my name."

So why did my "guidance" fail? For starters, we took an action and claimed "God told us" when He probably didn't. It was just our "slightly-out-of-whack" theology that required us to convince ourselves that it was all God's idea. Then, when it didn't work, we got stuck. We have to (1) blame God, or (2) attribute being stuck to character building, or (3) just simply remain stuck, having "faith" that God somehow will get us "unstuck."

What if we just admitted to ourselves that it's OK to pursue the passions of our hearts? God loves our initiative and promises to give us the desires of our hearts (Psalm 37:4). Then, when something goes wrong, we simply ask for His wisdom, make a mid-course correction, and move on. Here's where we really fail after something starts going wrong under the "obedience" approach to life. If we believed that "God told us to," we likely won't hear and make the mid-course correction! Why? If God didn't specifically guide us to start something, He's not going to provide the midcourse correction either. Now, God can interrupt us at any time with specifics and He occasionally does. But here's the norm, "He wants you to make specific, sanctified decisions, and all the mid-course corrections that are needed to make your dream successful." *You're* responsible—not God!

Be strong and of good courage. Would you like to know why Joshua got this admonition about eight different times? It's because God was inviting a leader to make some decisions, exercise some initiative, and take whatever land they chose on which to put their feet on. And the Holy Spirit is inviting you to do exactly the same thing.

> *I will give you every place where you set your foot, as*
> *I promised Moses.* (Joshua 1:3)

If you insist that God make all the decisions, as a symbol of your spirituality, you'll just get frustrated and hurt because He simply won't do it. If you choose to find the fortitude to take the responsibility to make wise decisions and make the adjustments that go with them, you start a great adventure and God will back you all the way.

> *If any of you lacks wisdom, he should ask God, who*
> *gives generously to all without finding fault, and it*
> *will be given to him. But when he asks, he must be-*
> *lieve and not doubt, because he who doubts is like a*

wave of the sea, blown and tossed by the wind. That man should not think he will receive anything from the Lord; he is a double-minded man, unstable in all he does. (James 1:5–8)

If you doubt that God wants you to ask for wisdom and then make decisions, life will blow you around as a leaf in the wind . . . and so will the devil. The common denominator I see in Kings who have turned the corner to receive God's favor is this: they make decisions and wield authority in the face of adversity. They don't get stuck or condemned, even if they fail. They just keep right on resurrecting, making wise decisions, wielding authority, getting blessed, and blessing others out of their overflow . . . and they have fun doing it.

Therefore, there is now no condemnation for those who are in Christ Jesus, because through Christ Jesus the law of the Spirit of life set me free. . . . (Romans 8:1–2)

Are you comfortable making decisions and asking "whatever?" If you are, the next obvious questions are, "How big a decision can I make? Is this initiative just for my own life or is there more?" God wants us to make wise personal decisions, but there is another level to which He's calling us—expanding the Kingdom. The scope of God's plans goes well beyond your personal life . . . and He's inviting us to participate in building the Kingdom with Him. We're called to bless the nations and God has not left us without the provisions to do that. Are you ready to get your heart's desires around that promise? More in the next chapter.

CHAPTER 4
BACK FROM THE FUTURE

Above all else, guard your heart, for it is the wellspring of life. (Proverbs 4:23)

Your heart is a wellspring. One of the great keys to spiritual health is the condition of our hearts. We usually think of that statement in the context of sin, but I want you to think of it in terms of the location of your heart. Many of us have projected our hearts into the future, and we have some verses to justify it. The result is that we're excited about what God is going to do in the future, but we're passive in the present. There are three distinct theological camps regarding this issue. See which one you're in.

Camp #1—The future is bleak; the rapture is our hope. People in this camp have great faith for Jesus' return, but often view themselves as a holy but persecuted remnant in terms of the present. They believe the enemy is in possession of many secular institutions, and the antichrist is behind the scenes manipulating events for evil. The newspapers are usually full of material to support this view. In Camp #1 hearts are projected all the way up to heaven, and they are not available to build the Kingdom now because everything in the present will be destroyed by future wars, famines, and earthquakes, or by the Lord Himself. In this camp my heart is positioned for hope in the rapture, and I keep it in neutral—"waiting" for the Savior. This camp tends to avoid entanglement with the "worldly" marketplace. Here's a verse I might use to distance myself from all the present carnality.

> *. . . Their mind is on earthly things. But our citizenship is in heaven. And we eagerly **await** a Savior from*

there, the Lord Jesus Christ, ...
(Philippians 3:19–20) [Emp. Added]

Camp #2—It's bad now, but revival is coming. This has been largely a position of the prophetic movement. Revivals, historically, and more recently in places such as Toronto, Canada, and Brownsville, Florida, remind us of God's ability to break out in power. So, we build our expectations around God's miraculous intervention and position our hearts to anticipate a revival in the future. Here's a verse we might use to point to God's future revival.

> *Come, and let us return unto the LORD: for He hath torn, and He will heal us; He hath smitten, and He will bind us up. After two days **will He revive us**: in the third day **He will raise us up**, and we shall live in His sight.*
> (Hosea 6:1–2) [Emp. Added]

Camp #3—The Kingdom is upon you. In this camp we see the Kingdom of God already established, and we see our role to expand it to fill the earth. It's not easy because the enemy does hold some territory, but it's our job to take it back. We also have many clear promises that we'll succeed. Our mentality is "we're winning," and our hearts are positioned in the present to make a difference.

Please hear this: We don't have to discount a coming revival or rapture; those are just not the primary focus of our heart—we're no longer "waiting." We're no longer "prophetic doomsayers."

The Kingdom of God is present on earth now. Those who can see it can expand it. My heart is positioned in the present to make a difference today. I'm back from the future; excited, empowered, and optimistic about the present. These are some of the verses I might use to point to the Kingdom of God.

> *But if I cast out devils by the Spirit of God, then the kingdom of God is come unto you.*
> (Matthew 12:28 KJV)

The Law and the Prophets were proclaimed until John; since that time the gospel of the kingdom of God has been preached, and everyone is forcing his way into it. (Luke 16:16 NASU)

No, in all these things we are more than conquerors through him who loved us.

(Romans 8:37 NIV)

The wellspring starts to flow. I get my heart back from the future and realize that I can do all things God has put in my heart through Christ *now* (Philippians 4:13). Instead of waiting on God for the next big thing, I actually can become more Christ-like and start making some things happen now in my own world. My heart is released to do its job . . . to create, to take initiative, to be bold and entrepreneurial, and to bear fruit. I look for opportunities, knowing they exist. My expectation is to be blessed by God so I'm positioned to bless the nations.

Walk with me. I was raised in a sleepy little Methodist church in a small town in Montana. As a child growing up, it gave me a foundation and an awareness of God, and I liked some of the songs (hymns). The Holy Spirit brought one back to mind this week. "In the Garden" was written in 1913 by Charles Austin Miles. In that hymn is a phrase I still can hear plainly, "He walks with me and He talks with me."

God is raising Kings who relate to him in a slightly different way. I'm not "waiting for" Him to do something big. I'm not just "waiting on" Him, as an obedient servant afraid of personal initiative. We're being elevated to "walk with Him" and "talk with Him." It's not a small change . . . it's more a revolution in terms of your prayer life, your heart's wellspring, and the fruit that will result. It's the level of relationship for which your heart was designed. It's the level of relationship for which the heart of God longs. Please don't wait. Doors are open for you to walk *with* the Lord, instead of *behind* Him, and experience new levels of prosperity and ministry. It's exciting.

The LORD would speak to Moses face to face, as a man speaks with his friend. (Exodus 33:11)

*I no longer call you servants, because a servant does not know his master's business. Instead, **I have called you friends, for everything that I learned from My Father I have made known to you**. You did not choose me, but I chose you and appointed you to go and bear fruit—fruit that will last. Then the Father will give you whatever you ask in my name.*
(John 15:15–17) [Emp. Added]

What's next? What is God's next move? Indeed we should ask that question and understand the times and seasons. But, God is asking a different question: "What's your next move?" Start the conversation.

At Gibeon the LORD appeared to Solomon during the night in a dream, and God said, "Ask for whatever you want Me to give you." (I Kings 3:5)

See also Matthew 7: 7–8; Matthew 20:21; Mark 10:36; Mark 11:24; Luke 18:41; John 14:13–14; John 15:16; John 16:23–24; James 1: 5–6; I John 5:14–15.

So I say to you: Ask and it will be given to you; seek and you will find; knock and the door will be opened to you. For everyone who asks receives; he who seeks finds; and to him who knocks, the door will be opened.
(Luke 11:9–10)

CHAPTER 5
WHEN WILL THY KINGDOM COME?

Painted with a broad brush—In 2005 we went to the Netherlands, and a well-meaning couple e-mailed me a half dozen times asking if I was "Kingdom Now" (a movement that got off track about 25 years ago). I did my best to explain that we don't emphasize covering nor crave authority over people or pastors. I went on to give a thorough history of the "Kingdom Now" movement in the U.S. in an attempt to distance myself from its imbalances in authority and doctrine. All for naught, of course. I was still "Kingdom Now" in their eyes, and they worked fairly hard to discourage people from coming to our meetings. It didn't particularly bother me, and I imagined that if I had roots in the World War II experience in that part of Europe, I might be a little sensitive about authority issues, as well.

Now or later? Since then, I've been re-reading old newsletter topics and writing new ones. Guess what? I keep running into a yearning to see the Kingdom of God "now." Ditto regarding all the above imbalances. Here are your choices: (1) you can put the Kingdom of God after the Second Coming, or (2) you can believe its available now. I've chosen the latter in this sense. I believe that after we're saved, our primary function isn't to revisit the cross every Sunday, while we wait for the rapture. We're here to possess our land and fill the earth with the glory of God. The Kingdom of God is not filling the earth at the moment, but it's our job to cooperate with God's plan to bring it down from heaven to earth, at least in part, before Jesus returns. I can see the theory of how people fall into setting up a religious hierarchy (theocracy), and make going to church the moral equivalent of joining the marines. However, I don't see God's people doing that these days. What is evident is a great liberation for saints who choose to receive their inheritance now and exercise faith in action to make it happen. Their ministries in the marketplace are fruitful spiritually and prosperous financially. Those waiting for the rapture are preoccupied with seeing the devil in every headline and miss the Kingdom entirely . . . just as the Pharisees of Jesus' day. They will be in heaven, I'm sure; they just will miss some of the fun of building the Kingdom on earth.

> *Therefore I tell you that the kingdom of God will be taken away from you and given to a people who will produce its fruit.* (Matthew 21:43)

The Kingdom in Luke—What really pushed me over the edge recently was re-reading the gospel of Luke and marking what Jesus said or did regarding the Kingdom. Here's what I found:

Jesus spoke of the Kingdom in the present tense all the time and He instructed His disciples to preach the gospel of the Kingdom.

> *. . . and He will reign over the house of Jacob forever; His kingdom will never end.* (Luke 1:33)

> *I must preach the good news of the kingdom of God to the other towns also, because that is why I was sent.* (Luke 4:43)

> *Blessed are you who are poor, for yours is the kingdom of God.* (Luke 6:20)

> *After this, Jesus traveled about from one town and village to another, proclaiming the good news of the kingdom of God.* (Luke 8:1)

Then, just as now, not everybody quite "gets it."

> *He said, "The knowledge of the secrets of the kingdom of God has been given to you, but to others I speak in parables, so that, 'though seeing, they may not see;*

though hearing, they may not understand.' "
(Luke 8:10)

Experiencing the power of the Kingdom is connected to healing and the miraculous. Calming the stormy sea is a great example of Jesus operating in the power of His Kingdom—already present.

> *. . . and he sent them out to preach the kingdom of God and to heal the sick.* (Luke 9:2)

> *He welcomed them and spoke to them about the kingdom of God, and healed those who needed healing.* (Luke 9:11)

Jesus told people they would see and experience the Kingdom before death.

> *. . . I tell you the truth, some who are standing here will not taste death before they see the kingdom of God.* (Luke 9:27)

> *Jesus said to him, "Let the dead bury their own dead, but you go and proclaim the kingdom of God."* (Luke 9:60)

> *Jesus replied, "No one who puts his hand to the plow and looks back is fit for service in the kingdom of God."* (Luke 9:62)

> *Heal the sick who are there and tell them, The kingdom of God is near you.* (Luke 10:9)

Jesus taught us to pray for the Kingdom to come . . . now. He wasn't advocating that people pray for 3000 years before the rapture comes. The power of God for healing and deliverance is evidence that the Kingdom is operating now, at least in many camps. God is pleased to "give His people the Kingdom."

*He said to them, "When you pray, say: 'Father, hallowed be Your name, **Your kingdom come**.'"*

(Luke 11:2) [Emp. added]

*But if I drive out demons by the finger of God, then **the kingdom of God has come to you**.*

(Luke 11:20) [Emp. added]

*But seek His kingdom, and these things will be given to you as well. "Do not be afraid, little flock, for **your Father has been pleased to give you the kingdom**."*

(Luke 12:31–33) [Emp. added]

Once people find out that the Kingdom is available to inherit *now*, there really is a "jailbreak" liberation to get involved. It's fun and fulfilling and exactly the plan of God. The Kingdom starts within you—you have to believe its available now to see it in operation.

The Law and the Prophets were proclaimed until John. Since that time, the good news of the kingdom of God is being preached, and everyone is forcing his way into it. (Luke 16:16)

Once, having been asked by the Pharisees when the kingdom of God would come, Jesus replied, "The kingdom of God does not come with your careful observation, nor will people say, 'Here it is,' or 'There it is,' because the kingdom of God is within you."

(Luke 17:20–21)

What is the most important criteria actually to enter the Kingdom now? You simply have to exercise a little childlike faith and believe it's possible for God to want you to heal the sick, cast out demons, prosper financially, change the world . . . etc.

Let the little children come to me, and do not hinder them, for the kingdom of God belongs to such as these.

I tell you the truth, anyone who will not receive the kingdom of God like a little child will never enter it.
(Luke 18:16–17)

We don't finish receiving the Kingdom in its fullest sense until Jesus' return. The concept of the Jewish belief at the time was that Jesus would return immediately and set up His own Kingdom to rule and reign.

While they were listening to this, he went on to tell them a parable, because He was near Jerusalem and the people thought that the kingdom of God was going to appear at once. (Luke 19:11)

And I confer on you a kingdom, just as my Father conferred one on me, so that you may eat and drink at my table in my kingdom and sit on thrones, judging the twelve tribes of Israel. (Luke 22:29–30)

So What? If you believe the Kingdom is later, you'll wait for it. If you believe it's available now, you'll contend for it. Does this little slant on theology make a difference? Yes, in practice it makes all the difference. Those in marketplace ministry have embraced it and are running with it. Building the Kingdom is the foundation for an entrepreneurial heart. It even touches the way we present the good news of the gospel. It isn't just about sin and the solution Jesus provided on the cross. It's about His resurrection and living life more abundantly. Kings who are examples and ambassadors of this gospel get a hearing without saying a word. Our slant on the Kingdom influences the way we articulate the good news of the gospel, as we'll explain in the next chapter.

CHAPTER 6
THE GOSPEL OF THE KINGDOM

After writing *Releasing Kings* and rethinking much of my Christian life, I'm excited about the message of the gospel. The "Good News" I used to share was a traditional message, similar to the Four Spiritual Laws. That is:

1. We are all sinners (*For all have sinned and fall short of the glory of God*—Romans 3:23)

2. We not only have sinned but we have sinful tendencies and sinful hearts (*Jesus came into the world to save sinners; of whom I am chief.*—I Timothy 1:15 KJV)

3. We need to invite Jesus into our lives and surrender our personal ambition (e.g., bring our sinful nature to "death") (*I have been crucified with Christ and I no longer live, but Christ lives in me*—Galatians 2:20).

4. We can look forward to and have confidence in going to heaven.

5. God has a wonderful plan for our lives.

What people hear from that message is that basically they are bad and that God hates sin and probably doesn't like them very much, either. What we communicated is that people are evil, they need to get saved and forsake all their selfish aspirations. Some of the verses we used were:

> *Then Jesus said to his disciples, "If anyone would come after me, he must deny himself and take up his cross*

and follow me. For whoever wants to save his life will lose it, but whoever loses his life for me will find it.
                                                (Matthew 16:24–25)

I have been crucified with Christ and I no longer live, but Christ lives in me. (Galatians 2:20)

Or don't you know that all of us who were baptized into Christ Jesus were baptized into His death? We were therefore buried with Him through baptism into death in order that, just as Christ was raised from the dead through the glory of the Father, we too may live a new life. (Romans 6: 3–4)

The Lemon Juice Gospel—There's nothing wrong with this message except that it stops short of any incentive to implement it. That's why traditional churches are in decline—the message doesn't resonate with what the Holy Spirit already is saying to people. Christianity is different because Jesus is alive and interactive, and the Holy Spirit has an influence on the present that we can see. We don't just speak words to people. When we share a more Bible-based gospel, the Holy Spirit causes the message to resonate in people so that they really are hearing God, instead of just us.

Guess what? God isn't telling most unsaved people that they are evil and have sinful aspirations. He's telling them He loves them, created them in His image, and their hearts' desires overlap with His plan for their lives. Some have sin issues, but many more have good desires, and they are basically good people. The sin emphasis in our message is true, but it's not the biggest problem most people face in meeting Jesus. The background theology is in Harold Eberle's book, *Precious in His Sight.* I recommend it highly.

Incentive—Why do I want to get saved? It's not just about heaven. God has an inheritance for us *now!* It's called the Kingdom. When we pursue God, the windows of heaven open, we're blessed, and we bless others. It's much more exciting than "sitting" and "waiting." The Kingdom starts now.

*Then the King will say to those on his right, Come, you who are blessed by my Father; **take your inheritance, the kingdom prepared for you** since the creation of the world.*

(Matthew 25:34) [Emp. Added]

*Do not fear, little flock, for **it is your Father's good pleasure to give you the kingdom.***

(Luke 12:32 NKJV) [Emp. Added]

*Therefore, since **we are receiving a kingdom that cannot be shaken**, let us be thankful, and so worship God acceptably with reverence and awe.*

(Hebrews 12:28) [Emp. Added]

Being Born Again lets us get our first glimpse of the Kingdom we'll inherit.

In reply Jesus declared, "I tell you the truth, no one can see the kingdom of God unless he is born again."

(John 3:3)

Baptism—As we're baptized and receive the Holy Spirit, we can enter the Kingdom we'll inherit. Being born again, baptized, and receiving the Holy Spirit are the keys that let us in the door of the Kingdom—not the goal.

Jesus answered, "I tell you the truth, no one can enter the kingdom of God unless he is born of water and the Spirit."

(John 3:5)

The Church Has the Keys. Note Matthew 16:18–19, Jesus gave the keys (salvation, baptism, etc.) of the Kingdom to the Church. The role of the Church is to equip the saints for the work of the ministry (Ephesians 4:11–12). But the "ministry" of saints called to be Kings is out in the Kingdom, not inside the walls of the Church. When we're "equipped," we have the power to unlock heaven's blessing and expand the Kingdom of God on earth.

And I tell you that you are Peter, and on this rock I will build my church, and the gates of Hades will not overcome it. **I will give you the keys** *of the kingdom of heaven; whatever you bind on earth will be bound in heaven, and whatever you loose on earth will be loosed in heaven.*

(Matthew 16:18–19) [Emp. Added]

The gospel of the Kingdom—After Jesus' death there was a huge emphasis on the Kingdom or the "Gospel of the Kingdom." That was the primary message of Good News . . . not just the death and burial (with which we identify in salvation and baptism) but the resurrection life, where we live out our Christian life.

After his suffering, he showed himself to these men and gave many convincing proofs that he was alive. He appeared to them over a period of forty days and **spoke about the kingdom of God**.

(Acts 1:3) [Emp. Added]

But when they believed Philip as he **preached the good news of the kingdom** *of God and the name of Jesus Christ, they were baptized, both men and women.* (Acts 8:12–13) [Emp. Added]

. . . We must go through many hardships to **enter the kingdom of God,** *. . .*

(Acts 14:22) [Emp. Added]

Paul entered the synagogue and spoke boldly there for three months, arguing persuasively about the **kingdom of God.**

(Acts 19:8) [Emp. Added]

They arranged to meet Paul on a certain day, and came in even larger numbers to the place where he

> *was staying. From morning till evening he explained and* **declared to them the kingdom of God** *and tried to convince them about Jesus from the Law of Moses and from the Prophets.*
>
> (Acts 28:23) [Emp. Added]

> *Boldly and without hindrance* **he preached the kingdom of God** *and taught about the Lord Jesus Christ.*
>
> (Acts 28:31) [Emp. Added]

What's the message of the Kingdom?

1. **You have an inheritance!** There's an inheritance for us in this life. We do have to be saved, etc., but the glass is "half full"—actually it's a cup running over. The Kingdom is much more than a life of duty and sacrifice, followed by eternal life after we die.

> *"I tell you the truth," Jesus replied, "no one who has left home or brothers or sisters or mother or father or children or fields for me and the gospel will fail to* **receive a hundred times as much in this present age** *(homes, brothers, sisters, mothers, children and fields—and with them, persecutions) and in the age to come, eternal life.*
>
> (Mark 10:29–30) [Emp. Added]

2. **You have power!** Once we're saved God equips us for the "work of the ministry" through our local church. We start co-laboring with Christ and doing the "works" outside the Church in the Kingdom.

> *I tell you the truth, anyone who has faith in me will do what I have been doing.* **He will do even greater things than these,** *because I am going to the Father. And I will do whatever you ask in my name, so that the Son may bring glory to the Father. You may ask me for anything in my name, and I will do it.*
>
> (John 14:12–14) [Emp. Added]

> *For the kingdom of God is **not a matter of talk but of power**.* (I Corinthians 4:20) [Emp. Added]

3. You have God's Heart! God has imprinted us with His own heart so that our hearts' desires match His. It's His goal to give us the desires of our hearts.

> *Delight yourself in the LORD and **He will give you the desires of your heart**.*
>
> (Psalm 37:4) [Emp. Added]

> *This is the covenant I will make with the house of Is-rael after that time, declares the Lord. **I will put my laws in their minds and write them on their hearts**. I will be their God, and they will be my people.*
>
> (Hebrews 8:10) [Emp. Added]

4. We're winners! The real emphasis of the "gospel" seen in its biblical entirety is not just death, burial, repentance, surrender, trials, and persecution (although we don't deny any of those things); it's also being victorious overcomers, healing the sick, raising the dead, casting out demons, et al.

> *As you go, preach this message: "'The kingdom of heaven is near.'" Heal the sick, raise the dead, cleanse those who have leprosy, drive out demons. Freely you have received, freely give.*
>
> (Matthew 10: 7–8)

5. We bless others! The gospel of the Kingdom also means learning to receive and use wealth for ministry. We're called to bless the nations.

> *But remember the LORD your God, for it is he who gives you the ability to produce wealth, and so con-firms his covenant, which he swore to your forefathers, as it is today.* (Deuteronomy 8:17–18)

> *I will make you into a great nation and I will bless*

you; I will make your name great, and you will be a blessing. I will bless those who bless you, and whoever curses you I will curse; and all peoples on earth will be blessed through you.

(Genesis 12: 2–3)

Will bad things happen? Of course, but it's not your commitment, self-discipline, or strength of character that will see you through them. It's the "joy set before you" . . . not just heaven, but all of your inheritance in the Kingdom in this life. Yes, you have a cross to bear, but it's pretty light compared with every good thing God has put in front of you.

*Let us fix our eyes on Jesus, the author and perfecter of our faith, who **for the joy set before him endured the cross**, scorning its shame, and sat down at the right hand of the throne of God. Consider him who endured such opposition from sinful men, so that you will not grow weary and lose heart.*

(Hebrews 12: 2–3) [Emp. Added]

***Consider it pure joy**, my brothers, whenever you face trials of many kinds, because you know that the testing of your faith develops perseverance.*

(James 1: 2–3) [Emp. Added]

*The apostles left the Sanhedrin, **rejoicing because they had been counted worthy of suffering disgrace for the name**. Day after day, in the temple courts and from house to house, they never stopped teaching and proclaiming the good news that Jesus is the Christ.*

(Acts 5:41–42) [Emp. Added]

And the good news is . . . Instead of just warning people about how hard it is to be a Christian and how bad they are, tell them how good Jesus is and how blessed they will be by their inheritance in the Kingdom. That's when your presentation of the gospel really will be balanced.

"Sin" isn't the biggest problem most people face right now. The biggest issue that weighs on their hearts is "Why am I here?" My neighbors aren't drug-dealing, wife-swappers destined for skid row and prison. They are hard working, married, and have kids that get good grades . . . but they are lost with respect to finding the adventure, passion, romance, joy, and meaning that God designed their hearts to experience. You see, sin is just a third-rate substitute for the eternal pleasures of knowing Jesus that begin when we get saved.

> *You have made known to me the path of life; you will*
> *fill me with joy in your presence, with eternal plea-*
> *sures at your right hand.*   (Psalm 16:11)

"A relationship with Jesus" is the answer to: "Why am I here?" A picture of everything God is doing with His people in the Kingdom is liberating, exciting, romantic . . . an adventure filled with the tempest of warfare, the thrill of heroism, the camaraderie of friends, and the generosity of abundance. Each of us has a unique and specific inheritance that we can choose to possess right now. Choose life . . . in fact, choose abundant life. Let the Lord overflow your cup so much that others get blessed, too.

Your next question might be, "How does all this appear in real life?" Glad you asked. More in the next chapter.

CHAPTER 7
IT LOOKS THIS WAY!

Howard—I had the opportunity to interview a great example of a King moving in the Kingdom (see <u>www.releasing-kings.com/Howard-Ferris.html</u>). If you would like to see the same package in a woman, let me introduce you to Dawnya Sasse (<u>www.releasing-kings.com/Dawnya-Sasse.html</u>).

Howard is an engineer who has been using his vacation and personal finances to provide crusade meetings for people who never have heard the gospel in Costa Rica, South America, and India. He's a natural evangelist! Here's a note I wrote from our phone conversation.

> Howard always has carried a sense that someday the Church would recognize his evangelistic ministry and help him go on crusades. He hoped that one day he would be invited to full-time ministry. Howard is 53 now and the invitation never came. Reading *Releasing Kings* helped Howard to realize that's OK; the resources of heaven come to Kings directly. The invitation did come—directly from God—because Howard decided to "go" instead of "sit."

Waiting for permission from the Church—We could write that same paragraph and hit 95% of all the Kings I've ever met. Sadly, many more still are sitting in the pews waiting for others to recognize their giftings and help them get started in a pulpit ministry inside the Church.

It's not the pastor's fault. After a few decades, many get a little "tude" and start to think it never will happen . . . and if you keep waiting, it never will! See, it's not really the pastor's responsibility to tell you "what and when" regarding your ministry. If you can't figure that out on your own, between you and God, then you really are not ready. I do wish we could stop the "bait and switch" phenomenon that is occurring currently. We do preach that ministries should be matured and sent—it's just that they seldom are. I think most pastors are wearied by all the initiatives eager beavers throw their way for decisions or funding. God is asking you to get the direction, make the decision, and bring the resources down out of heaven yourself.

Pass the test. The open view of God is simply this: God has left part of the future open for you to play a role in determining. Neither God nor your pastor is going to spell out every detail for you. It's decision time and you get to decide when you're ready to come off the bench (pew) and get in the game. Odds are good that your "game" is not even inside your local church. It's probably in the marketplace. Odds are even better that no one else is going to fund your ministry—especially not the local church where financing the building, staff, and missions commitments already have consumed 110% of the offerings.

Where does that leave you? Out in the cold? Actually, it leaves you right in the will of God. When you're willing to take the initiative, you will find an entrepreneurial anointing to multiply the resources and a door of ministry wide open in the marketplace. Kings are called to full-time ministry, anointed to multiply finances, and convert money into ministry.

Life after testing—Men and women find their ministry expressions in their marketplace vocations and take the presence and the power of God with them. Their deepest hearts' desires find expression in their entrepreneurial pursuits. They come alive. In fact, "life" starts when we start doing the things God created us to do. Get it? Entrepreneurial expression leads to prosperity, which leads to life. Our cup overflows and ministry is the result (helping others through the same process). That 40-hour ministry is the one that will expand the Kingdom and reach the world. Can you see that it's spiritual to be entrepreneurial? He's the God of

Abraham, Isaac, and Jacob (all businessmen).

The Church is there to equip us until we "pass the test." Ministry is in the Kingdom. When we're saved we're translated into the Kingdom of God. We're equipped for ministry in the Church, and then we "work" or minister in the Kingdom.

> *For he has rescued us from the dominion of darkness and brought us into the kingdom . . .*
> (Colossians 1:13 NIV)

> *. . . my fellow **workers** for the kingdom of God. . . .*
> (Colossians 4:11) [Emp. Added]

Take the test! It's open book and open view. Before we really can give ourselves permission to experience the emotion of true passion, we have to be convinced that God is OK with getting that excited. Are you ready for passion? The next section is all about how.

PART I
I'M PROPHETIC—GOD AND I TALK
THOUGHT QUESTIONS AND EXERCISES

Business people who don't yet know the Lord, are confident and directed in what they want. As Christians, and those called to do exploits in this hour, we need to get comfortable with the grace God has already put in our hearts.

1. Why do you feel you are somewhat tentative to articulate and believe what's in your heart?

2. Sometimes a theological worldview blocks our progress. Is there anything in your past experience or Christian heritage that confuses your heart? What are they?

3. Once you push those aside, what do you really believe God's already told you that's unique to you?

4. Getting in touch with what God has put in your heart can take dialogue with God. How do you connect at this level? Ask Him questions and try to write down the answers.

5. Imagine God invited you to co-author the script for your own movie / life where you were the main character. How good can you make it? How much adventure, favor, romance, and hero-ism would you put in it.

6. Did you know God stopped what He was doing, and watched Adam as he named the animals? This was the first ranching enterprise being born! Check it out in Genesis 2:19–20. Does this not suggest God will hang out with us as we pursue our God Exploits? How is your "hanging-out-with-God" experience? What can you do to make it more intimate and real?

Note: See the "Prophetic Insight-Starting with God" module at www.desiretodestiny.com. More resources and mentoring tools and services to help you on this adventure are available on our website under Mentoring and Coaching.

KEY II
I'M PASSIONATE—FOLLOWING
THE DESIRES OF MY HEART

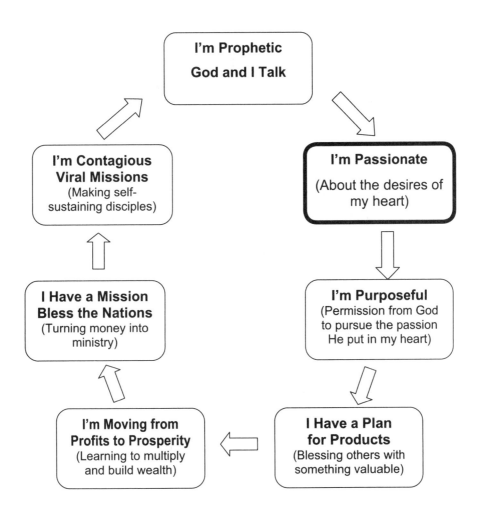

I'm Prophetic
God and I Talk

I'm Contagious
Viral Missions
(Making self-
sustaining disciples)

I'm Passionate
(About the desires of
my heart)

I Have a Mission
Bless the Nations
(Turning money into
ministry)

I'm Purposeful
(Permission from God
to pursue the passion
He put in my heart)

I'm Moving from
Profits to Prosperity
(Learning to multiply
and build wealth)

I Have a Plan
for Products
(Blessing others with
something valuable)

P assion is allowing yourself to experience the thrill of engaging your heart's desire . . . allowing your dream to come true. Passion comes with a few milestones that must be experienced (listed below, followed by a chapter devoted to each).

Like yourself. You are God's treasure; valuable enough to seek and find. You are His pearl worth enough to sell a field and buy. If you'll accept God's assessment of your person, you'll have to start liking yourself . . . and accepting the value of your heart's desires.

Be yourself. Like the lilies of the field, our job is to become ourselves. Religion is remaking yourself into something you're not. God is asking us to look into our desires and become what He created us to be.

Trust your heart. Once you start liking yourself and sifting through your heart's desires, you'll find God's fingerprints everyplace! Your passion is connected to your own initiative. You imagine greater accomplishments and instinctively enjoy the entrepreneurial process.

Plans—It's my biblical responsibility to build a plan around my dream and pursue it. Spiritual maturity is all about getting excited about your passion/dream.

Encourage your heart. You can encourage your heart by allowing yourself to emulate someone who already is doing your passion. "Healthy envy" is a signal that God is activating the passion of your heart.

Manage your dream. What happens when our dream starts to crash? We have to get busy and manipulate the script. We "manage" the outcome via prayer, midcourse corrections, the power of God, and persistence so we land on our heart's desire.

Ask. All of us go through periods of waiting for a desire to materialize. So does God. Our hunger and God's assurance cause us to ask and keep on asking. We just don't and won't give up.

Try. Our hearts and minds are places where God writes His plan. This is one of the great promises of regeneration that God is powerful enough to accomplish. A dream or a desire goes from theory to practice when we try.

CHAPTER 8
YOU'RE A TREASURE

One of the key ingredients required before you can "inherit" your heart's desires and embrace your passion is that you simply have to "like yourself." God does. In fact, He considers you a treasure.

> *The kingdom of heaven is like treasure hidden in a field. When a man found it, he hid it again, and then in his joy went and sold all he had and bought that field.*　　　　　　　　(Matthew 13:44 NIV)

Treasures—The traditional view of this parable is that the Kingdom is the Treasure, and we should sell all to obtain it. Jesus is the man who found a treasure (you) in a field (the world), and in His joy He "bought us with a price." (I Corinthians 6:20) This view helps us have God's perspective on our own lives. "Sinners saved by grace" is true but doesn't completely describe who we are in God's eyes. We're a treasure that brought joy to God's heart and caused Him to pay the highest possible price to redeem us. God personally takes delight in you and rejoices over you!

> *No longer will they call you Deserted, or name your land Desolate. But you will be called Hephzibah, and your land Beulah; for **the LORD will take delight in you**, and your land will be married. As a young man marries a maiden, so will your sons marry you; as a bridegroom rejoices over his bride, **so will your God rejoice over you**.*
>
> (Isaiah 62: 4–5) [Emp. Added]

You're valuable. Many commentators worry that the "man" was dishonest; he failed to tell the owner about the treasure before he bought the field. The reality is that we were of no value to anyone but God. The devil certainly doesn't place any value on you and most of the world doesn't either. What I'm realizing is that once we enter the Kingdom (or have the Kingdom in us), we can see people through God's eyes. They are treasures, already purchased, and waiting to be esteemed the way God sees them.

The next parable repeats the same message. The pearl isn't the Kingdom that we buy. Your works don't buy anything. You are the pearl purchased by Jesus because of the value He sees in you.

> *Again, the kingdom of heaven is like a merchant looking for fine pearls. When he found one of great value, he went away and sold everything he had and bought it.* (Matthew 13:45–46)

When you like yourself you're naturally more comfortable seeing yourself the way God does—favored and blessed. You're much more likely to pursue the desires of your heart and try new things. Here's the "rule of thumb." You act on the outside the way you feel about yourself on the inside. Are you a forgiven sinner? You'll barely get by. Are you a treasure and a pearl, favored by God to "more than conqueror" status? That's how you will act.

When the Kingdom is in you—When Jesus spoke to the Pharisees they were anticipating a natural kingdom and missing the fact that the Kingdom already was present. Similarly, many of us have been waiting for the rapture, hoping for the kingdom to come, and missing that fact that it's already here.

> *Once, having been asked by the Pharisees when the kingdom of God would come, Jesus replied, "The kingdom of God does not come with your careful observation, nor will people say, 'Here it is,' or 'There it is,' because the kingdom of God is within you."* (Luke 17:20–21)

Examples—I'm privileged to meet many of God's people who have the Kingdom within them. They are ministering in the marketplace as Kings, and they've got this "Kingdom" thing operating; an army of people who are being raised up right now for the Kingdom.

God is opening my eyes to see the joy He has over them. Plus, there are certain distinctives that make them standout as peculiar treasures, zealous of good works. When I say "zealous of good works," they are not earning salvation, but they are having a great time co-laboring with Christ.

> *Who gave himself for us, that He might redeem us from all iniquity, and purify unto Himself **a peculiar people, zealous of good works.***
> (Titus 2:14—KJV) [Emp. Added]

TEN EXPRESSIONS OF THE "KINGDOM WITHIN YOU"

See if you can spot some "Kings" you know in the following ten characteristics. They truly are treasures and they are no longer hidden. More importantly, can you see yourself?

1. **Networking**—There is an amazing synergism that leads those who operate with a Kingdom mentality to find one another and the opportunities for increase and ministry. It's as if God were leading them!

2. **Heart's desires**—These folks are creatively moving toward their hearts' desires. They love what they do and find ministry in the course of doing it. They are entrepreneurial as a result.

3. **Vision**—They have given themselves permission to pursue a portion of the kingdom they understand to be their "land" or assignment. They don't expect their pastors to define their ministries or the will of God for them.

4. **Enthusiasm**—They are excited about their lives and fueled by the experience of being personally used by God to bless others

and build the Kingdom. They already hear, "Well done, good and faithful servant."

5. **Abundance**—They have given themselves permission to prosper financially; they have practical means to make it happen; they have a plan to convert their resources into ministry and lay up treasure in heaven. Poverty mentality is absent.

6. **Favor**—They expect blessing. They have an amazing string of "coincidences" pointing to God's favor on their lives.

7. **Persistence**—They experience their fair share of problems, but they never are defeated by them. They just find a way around or through them. Trouble never fazes their belief that God will carry them through. They find opportunities in obstacles. They joyfully resurrect once after every death . . . as a way of life.

8. **Fun loving**—They know how to play, dream, take vacations, and not take themselves too seriously. They act as God's kids on a great adventure that can't go wrong. They love to promote others to their levels of blessing or more.

9. **Witnessing**—An amazing number of them can preach and teach, but they are neither preachy, condescending, nor compelled to cast others in the mold of sinners needing to repent. They attract unbelievers by the favor on their lifestyles and by being personable. Unsaved people start to see themselves as treasures when exposed to this crowd.

10. **Beyond Prophetic**—They converse with Jesus "face-to-face." Their concept of responding to God is not merely obedience but partnership. They operate out of a sense of doing what the Father is doing, and they are not afraid to take initiative and fill in the blanks associated with knowing the general will of God. They are not afraid of mistakes and view midcourse adjustments as a normal part of their co-adventure with Jesus. They interact with the person of God, not just the direction of God nor Words from God, nor the work of God.

*"When a prophet of the L*ORD *is among you, I reveal myself to him in visions, I speak to him in dreams. But this is not true of my servant Moses; he is faithful in all my house. With him I speak face to face, clearly and not in riddles; he sees the form of the L*ORD.*"*

(Numbers 12: 6–8)

I no longer call you servants, because a servant does not know his master's business. Instead, I have called you friends, for everything that I learned from my Father I have made known to you.

(John 15:15 NIV)

See, you are a treasure to God and to those around you. Now let's see if we can let you become more like you! Be yourself.

CHAPTER 9
BECOMING "YOU" (MATTHEW 6)

The single greatest key to Kingly marketplace ministry is finding out who you are and simply being yourself. Matthew 6 is all about "seeking first the Kingdom and His righteousness." It sets off a dynamic where everything else is added quite naturally. Here's the simple goal; take inventory of your desires and talents and find the synergism with the will of God. You have to believe that God created you with the right tools to fulfill His plan and your entire destiny. I used to believe being "kingdom oriented" meant you lay down your life, surrender all your ambition, and give yourself as a servant, doing what you don't really enjoy because you love the Lord . . . that was the "good news of the gospel." You may start there, but you can't end there. Jesus came so that you could have life. You'll have to lay down sin, but the gospel is really all about picking up life. To be good at life you have to enjoy life and be yourself. Otherwise it's just a pharisaic version of religion . . . something Jesus resisted with vigor. "Christ in you" is the hope of glory.

> *To them God has chosen to make known among the Gentiles the glorious riches of this mystery, which is **Christ in you, the hope of glory.***
> (Colossians 1:27) [Emp. Added]

Storing treasure in heaven—(Matthew 6:19–24) Much of Christianity is quite smug about staying in poverty. They view people with the work ethic and wisdom to accumulate wealth as though they are far from God. In reality, "poor in spirit" reflects a receiving attitude. Prosperity begins when we learn how to receive from God. We learn how to receive from mentors with wealth. Christians are just starting to come out from under the "I'm-too-spiritual-for-wealth" mentality. Here's where it's headed: some day soon we'll define "spiritual" in terms of our entrepreneurial initiative and our ability to multiply the favor of God to do exploits.

Do we worship wealth? No, we can't take it with us. Wealth is just a tool that makes ministry possible. We can convert money into ministry and store treasure in heaven. That's what Kings do; they get so blessed they can be a blessing (Genesis 12: 2–3). We don't serve money; money serves us as a tool to build the Kingdom.

Why worry? (Matthew 6:25–35) You would expect Kings to be encumbered with a Martha spirit that is a crowded schedule and a plate full of things about which to worry. On the contrary, just as the birds and the lilies we simply live out our hearts' desires and God takes care of us by opening door after door after door. It's hard to worry when you know your increase came from God. Sure, you worked hard but God multiplied. Worry is far from our real emotion about tomorrow. It's one of excitement and anticipation about what great breakthrough will overtake us next. OK, what about the down times? Same emotion; we just know God will overcome and resurrect us. We're unsinkable . . . even in death.

The dynamic (see how the lilies grow). What do birds and lilies have in common with us? Seeking the Kingdom first is really all about being yourself. God will multiply you the minute you stop trying to be something you're not . . . not a hypocrite . . . nothing for show. We're just finding our way into our hearts' desires and into the will of God. The result—we're blessed beyond Solomon. Don't spiritualize that away. Solomon was the wealthiest and wisest man on earth in his day and made a huge difference for the nation he led and served. That's the promise of finding yourself in God. Naturally you'll be energized and positioned to make a difference and have fun doing it.

> See how the lilies of the field grow. They do not labor
> or spin. Yet I tell you that not even Solomon in all his
> splendor was dressed like one of these. If that is how

*God clothes the grass of the field, which is here today
and tomorrow is thrown into the fire, will he not much
more clothe you, O you of little faith?*
(Matthew 6:28–30)

All these things will be added List 100 of your heart's desires; everything about which you have a passion. It won't take long to realize that all the houses, cars, boats, land, and possessions grow tiresome compared with co-laboring with God. God is so amazingly generous that He doesn't withhold possessions. But, the more we get to know Him, the more we want to "trade up" for the real treasures of the Kingdom. When you put the Kingdom first, you'll be amazed at how everything else aligns up. "All these things" show up, even though they are no longer on the top of your list.

*But seek first his kingdom and His righteousness, and
all these things will be given to you as well. Therefore do not worry about tomorrow, for tomorrow will
worry about itself. Each day has enough trouble of its
own.* (Matthew 6:33–34)

The next question is, "Where do I find this dynamite?" God wired it right inside your hearts' desires. Pretty amazing!

CHAPTER 10
FINDING GOD IN YOUR HEART

I've been impacted profoundly with the realization that my concepts of man and God were a half bubble off (see chapters 7–9 of *Releasing Kings* and *Precious in His Sight* by Harold Eberle). Here's the crux of the matter. If we believe "man" is inherently sinful, we will be led irrevocably to conclude the desires or passions in his heart are corrupt, as well. If we believe we were created in God's image, and that He can redeem whatever is corrupt and change our hearts, then we can be much more optimistic.

This quote came in an e-mail from a respected leader.

> One of these days a nurse will enter your intensive care unit, observe the flat signal on the electronic heart monitor, unplug the life-support system, and quietly walk out of the room. At that moment, you will find yourself in eternity face to face with God. One question He plans to ask you is **whether you shared the passions of His heart, or whether you followed your own.** How you answer that question will determine the quality of your existence for all eternity.

Hidden in the prose is a misconception we all should learn to recognize (easily). The Lord is showing Kings a place of finding the desires of their hearts that match His desires. The misconception in the above paragraph (and throughout much of Christianity) is that you have to forsake your own will to take God's will . . . you're either serving yourself or serving God. Here's the truth: God is big enough to create us in His own image with a thirst for goodness and draw us to Himself so that our desires match His.

What happens if you live in the either/or world of continually forsaking your own desires as carnal. That's a one-way ticket on a works trip. People ignite when they give themselves permission to pursue their passions. It's not spiritual at all to grovel in the inadequacy of human nature; we actually deny the power of God when we do. When we first come to the Lord, we do have to overcome carnal appetites and replace them with Godly desires. It's healthy to serve "that which is another man's." The day comes, however, when we have to identify and pursue the passion for which God created us. If you don't, you always live from paycheck to paycheck, both literally and in the bank account of your heart.

Most of us have been taught that our hearts are desperately wicked and an unreliable source for any kind of "guidance." Here are a few of the Scriptures the old John Garfield would have used to prove your heart is evil.

> The LORD smelled the pleasing aroma and said in his heart: "Never again will I curse the ground because of man, even though every inclination of his heart is evil from childhood." (Genesis 8:21)

> "For my thoughts are not your thoughts, neither are your ways my ways," declares the LORD." As the heavens are higher than the earth, so are my ways higher than your ways and my thoughts than your thoughts. (Isaiah 55: 8–9)

My view on those passages and others similar to them was tainted by my theological roots. Here's what I've come to realize. Our hearts or souls have to be discerned. There are lots of instances in the Bible where evil in men was discerned. That doesn't mean men are depraved totally and wicked all the time. God is in the process of redeeming our hearts and souls and conforming us to the image of Christ. We were created in God's image and redemption is all about living there. Now I'm quoting the rest of the Bible regarding our hearts. The world is full of good people with good hearts. Many good people still need to meet Jesus and are very open to finding salvation. They don't need to become sinners in order to be saved. They just need a relationship made possible by Jesus' death, burial, and resurrection.

Delight yourself in the LORD and he will give you the desires of your heart.

(Psalm 37:4)

He fulfills the desires of those who fear him; he hears their cry and saves them.

(Psalm 145:19)

If you remain in me and my words remain in you, ask whatever you wish, and it will be given you. This is to my Father's glory, that you bear much fruit, showing yourselves to be my disciples.

(John 15: 7–8)

God is leading many Kings through a thrilling process of getting connected with their hearts' desires. Here's the secret—you're going to find the will of God in your heart's desire. Sure you have to judge those desires and discern which are godly and which are not. But for Christians, the will of God goes through the desires of your hearts. I used to feel quite spiritual when I was doing something for God I didn't enjoy. Now, I'm still willing to sacrifice and live a disciplined life, but the reason is for the joy set before me . . . in this life. Kings love the will of God and delight in expanding the Kingdom. To be creative, entrepreneurial, fruitful, and prosperous is both naturally and spiritually the great adventure—Christianity.

Example: It's not a sacrifice to do the will of God and go do a conference in the Netherlands. It's a party, an adventure, and a thrill for me, and many were released as Kings in the process.

This is the covenant I will make with the house of Israel after that time, declares the Lord. I will put my laws in their minds and write them on their hearts. I

will be their God, and they will be my people.
(Hebrews 8:10)

That's the theology. But how do we make it practical. Jacob has a few hints.

1. Acknowledge your heart's desire. Jacob had a job working for his uncle that he did extremely well but didn't enjoy it very much. The desire of his heart was to get away from punching the clock and do something for his own family. Notice this transition.

> *The little you had before I came has increased greatly, and the LORD has blessed you wherever I have been. But now,* **when may I do something for my own household?** *(Genesis 30:30) [Emp. Added]*

The Holy Spirit has put this question in many Kings right now. You've worked for another man or corporation, you've been faithful, and now God wants to give you that which is your own. Something for your own household, instead of just prospering the company for which you work.

> *And if ye have not been faithful in that which is another man's, who shall give you that which is your own?* *(Luke 16:12 KJV)*

2. Weaned from wages—Laban didn't want to lose Jacob because he'd been a great employee for 14 years. Jacob entered the negotiation with a history of good performance. Instead of asking for a raise, Jacob says, "Don't give me anything" (Genesis 30:31) for wages!!! Pretty amazing! He could have asked for a raise, a pension, insurance, tenure, six weeks vacation, and a goat herder's union. Jacob is pursuing the desire of his heart through an entrepreneurial contract.

3. The business angle—Jacob now sets himself up in business through a contract with Laban. Note the business principles he employs:

    a. The dream—Jacob's desire to do something for his own household had a progression; *first a thought, then a dream, then a vi-*

sion, then a plan, then a change, then the practice, then reality.

b. **Quit his job**—Jacob's contract is performance based, and he is paid per goat instead of just selling his time on the job. Laban agrees that Jacob is going to keep all the spotted goats raised from the flock.

c. **Multiplication**—Jacob sets in motion a wealth-building principle of multiplication. The goats are now Jacob's employees, and they are multiplying his wealth with every new spotted kid. This is a key principle in building wealth. There is no particular advantage to starting a business over a job until you discover how to leverage your time, talents, money, and ideas to multiply your efforts. It's called "working smarter" instead of harder, and it's the command of Genesis 1:28: "Be fruitful and multiply."

d. **Entrepreneurial creativity**—Jacob also employs some new technology so that when the goats mate in front of some branches, the offspring are spotted (Genesis 30:37–42). He used anointed creativity to enhance his business. I'm not sure how this worked and I'm not aware that anyone in agriculture ever has duplicated Jacob's genetic science.

The results—After working for 14 years in a job at a subsistence level, where his employer changed his wages ten times (Gen 31:7), Jacob then became wealthy in the following six, short years. He still worked hard. But now he's working smarter and working for himself and God, instead of Laban.

> *In this way the man grew **exceedingly prosperous**
> and came to own large flocks, and maidservants and
> menservants, and camels and donkeys.*
> (Genesis 30:43) [Emp. Added]

God has breakthroughs in mind for you. Kings just need to learn to cultivate a Jacob-like pursuit of the blessing. "Exceedingly prosperous" is not an accident nor a miracle. It's the conscious plan of Spirit-filled people throughout the earth. We're called to be vessels through whom God can bless all nations. You'll have to be really blessed to fulfill your part of that promise. Go for it!

Where do I start? Translate your heart's desires into a plan of action.

CHAPTER 11
PLANS OF THE HEART

When we eventually learn to bring our prayer in this way, we often make the following ending.

"Lord, this is what we want, but there's one thing we want more than this. We want to be absolutely sure of being in the center of Your will. Therefore, we submit what we want under Your will. Let Your will be done. Amen."

As we have learned to pray this way, the Lord has answered our prayers every time in a very distinct way. **God requires us to morally own our decisions so that He can interact with us as adults rather than children who don't really know what they want.** He wants us to grow in authority and responsibility before Him to access His Kingdom privileges. (*Business Unlimited* by Gunnar Olson, p. 119)

Growing up—We all subscribe to the fact that authority in prayer begins with understanding the will of God. Knowing the will of God is closely tied to understanding the real desires of your heart. We should know what we want! God isn't particularly blessed by unthinking robots. He enjoys the maturity of children who have wills and share His desires from the depths of their own hearts.

Put your heart in gear. Most of us have been taught our need to surrender, wipe the slate clean, and otherwise eradicate every carnal desire of our hearts. Few know how to encourage the desires of their hearts and find the place where our desires and God's desires are one. I want to suggest something radical . . . no, biblical! Finding the will of God starts when you walk toward the desires of your heart. The whole concept of staying in neutral until you hear from God has roots in faulty theology, a belief that your heart is evil and full of carnal desires. God does steer us, tweak the plan, adjust the timing, etc. But we're the ones who offer the plan, discern it, commit it to the Lord, and proceed with it. He likes your initiative. Your will is not an enemy. It's a God-given gift, and the desires of your heart are "normally" an expression of something God put there, just as He promised, "I will put my laws in their hearts." (Hebrews 10:16)

> To man belong the **plans of the heart**, but from the LORD comes the reply of the tongue.
> (Proverbs 16:1) [Emp. Added]

> **In his heart a man plans his course**, but the LORD determines his steps.
> (Proverbs 16:9) [Emp. Added]

> Delight yourself in the LORD and He will give you the desires of your heart. **Commit your way** to the LORD; trust in Him and He will do this:
> (Psalm 37: 4–5) [Emp. Added]

> If the LORD delights in a **man's way**, He makes his steps firm; though he stumble, he will not fall, for the LORD upholds him with his hand.
> (Psalm 37:23–24) [Emp. Added]

When I previously read these verses, I could see only that God intervened and saved me from pursuit of my carnal desires. Now I can see what is plainly in the text: it is my responsibility to put together a plan based upon the desires of my heart . . . and, oh, by the way, they match God's desires.

Let my people go. Hearts must be discerned, discipled, counseled, mentored, and matured. But spiritual maturity begins when we give our hearts permission to dream and then make plans around those dreams. It's a different lifestyle. A religious spirit really is opposing your heart's desire and is trying to live out some notion of what God wants you to do (usually defined by others). One is oppressive, life-killing, bondage. But making a plan to live the dream God put in your heart is alive, creative, prosperous, contagious, generous, and fun.

> *Sacrifice and offering you did not desire; my ears you have opened. Burnt offering and sin offering you did not require. Then I said, "Behold, I come; In the scroll of the book it is written of me. I delight to do your will, O my God, And your law is within my heart."*
> (Psalm 40: 6–8 NKJV)

We delight to do your will, Lord. It's in our hearts.

Once you have a plan based upon your heart's desire, your passion will ignite. So will the warfare and the problems. Persistence is required, and you'll need to learn how to encourage your heart through obstacles—the topic of the next chapter.

CHAPTER 12
HOW TO ENCOURAGE YOUR HEART

*To man belong the **plans of the heart**, but from the LORD comes the reply of the tongue.*
                    (Proverbs 16:1) [Emp. Added]

Spiritual maturity is reaching a place where your heart's desire and the will of God become the same. Here are some practical tips on how to get there.

Healthy envy—One of the early signs that God is unveiling your heart's desire is that you see someone else doing your heart's desire . . . you'll be drawn to emulate that person. When you see someone with a calling, gifting, and anointing similar to your own, you naturally gravitate toward them. You'll experience a healthy envy that draws you into their anointing. They are examples the Lord is showing you to pull you into your own destiny. Let your envy work its way into mentoring. We are drawn into their anointing by the Holy Spirit. Godly mentors don't focus on accountability; they focus on making you a success and letting you hold yourself accountable to something that works. That's why we like to interview Kings and find mentors who already have tapped into an anointing for prosperity and ministry in the marketplace.

> ***Follow my example**, as I follow the example of Christic.*   (I Corinthians 11:1) [Emp. added]

> *. . . for in Christ Jesus I became your father through the gospel. Therefore I urge you to **imitate me**.*
>   (I Corinthians 4:15–16) [Emp. added]

*Join with others in **following my example**, brothers*
(Philippians 3:17) [Emp. added]

***You became imitators** of us and of the Lord. . . .*
(I Thessalonians 1:6) [Emp. added]

*We did this, not because we do not have the right to such help, but in order to make ourselves **a model for you to follow**.*
(II Thessalonians 3:9) [Emp. added]

*We do not want you to become lazy, but to **imitate** those who through faith and patience inherit what has been promised.*
(Hebrews 6:12) [Emp. added]

Unity vs unique Nearly all Christians learn to find themselves by serving in someone else's vision for a period of time. Many are called to support another's vision as their primary calling. It's the desire of their hearts. The desire of your heart, your calling, may be uniquely your own, or it may be shared with another group, your church, for example. I heard many imbalanced sermons on the evils of being a lone ranger with an independent spirit. At the time, we didn't believe in the concept of ministry outside the Church. Theologically, we had painted ourselves into a corner where entrepreneurs with business or ministry outside the Church were missing God. As a pastor, I was prone to preach the virtues of people who supported the church and worked with me to make it grow. I was silent on the need to expand the Kingdom in the marketplace outside the church. Now we know that God is using both priestly ministries to equip the saints and Kingly ministries to expand the Kingdom beyond the walls of the local church.

Graduating disciples—We should disciple new believers gradually to find their place in the Kingdom and/or in the Church. We also are winding our way around to a concept where we realize that the Church is a place to be equipped, but the marketplace is where ministry opportunities come for nearly all of us.

Fearing your heart—Instead of discerning our heart's desires to find the will of God, many Christians have no theological basis even to consider the possibility. We're steeped in concern over presumption, dead works, getting ahead of God, missing God, etc. That fear keeps us from hearing one of the primary ways God speaks; through our heart's desires. We've been taught that our voice of personal desire is carnal. We charismatics are great at unction, prophecy, still small voice, dreams, listening prayer, and fasting . . . we miss the forest for the trees. We miss hearing the desires God put in our hearts. When we're fearful of missing the will of God, we actually open a door to deception. We actually put too much weight on prophetic words or on the leadership of others. Don't get me wrong; God does use other people to lead us and give valid prophetic words. My point is that those ministries are intended to mature us to hear God ourselves. They should confirm what's already in our hearts.

You gotta ask! No one really has reached God's best by crucifying their heart's desires. It's really just a life-killing tradition in which most of us have been raised. Make a decision between you and God that you'll allow Him to give you the same invitation He gave Solomon, "Ask whatever." Notice when Solomon is finished with round one of his heart's desire (at Gibeon), God visits him again (at Gibeon). Can you see this is a normal pattern? We're supposed to ask! Solomon achieved what he had desired to do. Jesus made that point a dozen times in the New Testament.

> *At Gibeon the LORD appeared to Solomon during the night in a dream, and God said, "Ask for whatever you want me to give you."*
> (1 Kings 3:5) [Emp. added]

> *When Solomon had finished building the temple of the LORD and the royal palace, and had achieved all he had desired to do, the LORD appeared to him a second time, as he had appeared to him at Gibeon.*
> (1 Kings 9:1–3) [Emp. added]

Mistakes and home runs—We're not just fighting tradition. Most of us have stepped out on some ambition that did "go south." We all have stories of dead works, presumption, and failed initiatives. So what? It's called experience. If we vow never to trust our hearts again, we cut ourselves off from the deepest levels of intimacy with God. Want to know what makes God really mad? That servant who hid his talent because he was afraid of failure. Faith is "knowing in part," stepping out of the boat, and trusting a loving Father who longs for our initiative.

You really are called to be a hero, to hit the home run, to be a star. To be God's man or woman, you're going to have to take your best swing, best swings (plural). Ask and keep on asking. Swing and keep on swinging. I think the Lord and the devil agree on one thing. They both want to know what you're going to do after the first two strikes.

With all your heart—I used to think seeking and loving God with all my heart referred to intensity. Now I understand it's an important aspect of my relationship with God. He's asking me to go into the desires of my heart, encourage them, discern them, refine them, and operate out of them. He doesn't want my heart surrendered, abandoned, or crucified; He wants it to be alive, engaged, thrilled, motivated, and loved.

> *You will seek me and find me when you seek me with* ***all your heart****.*
>
> (Jeremiah 29:13) [Emp. added]

> *He answered: " 'Love the Lord your God with* ***all your*** *****heart*** and with all your soul and with all your strength and with all your mind'; and, 'Love your neighbor as yourself.' "*
>
> (Luke 10:27) [Emp. added]

Encourage the desires of your heart instead of quenching them. Allow yourself to get excited about your personal adventure with God. Will problems arise? Of course they will. Our response to those problems is simply to manage them so our passion is preserved . . . the topic of the next chapter.

Do you want those dreams to materialize? Decide now to "make them" a reality as we discuss in the next chapter.

CHAPTER 13
"MAKING" DREAMS COME TRUE

About ten years ago the author of a book on dreams spoke at our church. It heightened a healthy awareness of this avenue for the Holy Spirit to speak to us. As I began to record my dreams and pursue the interpretation, I also became more aware that some of my dreams seemed to have no redeemable features and were embarrassingly carnal or destructive—as if they were inspired more by the enemy than God. It bothered me for awhile until someone shared a handy little recipe (maybe it was the original speaker—honestly I've forgotten).

For the dreams that did seem to originate with the enemy, I would be half awake trying to discern the origin. Before I left that "alpha" state, I simply would rewrite the outcome so that God got the glory and the ending of the dream was a happy one. For some of them I had to rewind the tape and rewrite the ending. If there were a death, I would add a resurrection. If there were an accident, I added a scene where the Lord intervened at the last minute to prevent a disaster. In every case, I made the Lord a hero and myself a King. Seems to be like cheating, doesn't it? You know, I haven't had many dreams that needed to be rewritten since I learned to fix the outcome.

Now the Lord is teaching me another level. I have a dream (or vision) for my life. I want to be a King, help others to be Kings, live on 10%, and start a reformation that will touch the great commission through marketplace ministry. Just as in sleep dreams, the story line isn't always a good one, and I don't always feel as if I'm headed for a happy ending. As I look at my life and my occasional failures or delays, my logical mind and my natural fears start predicting a less-than-victorious future. The Lord is giving me the permission and power to change the ending. Even though I can't experience the future yet, I simply am praying, proclaiming, prophesying, and doing whatever resurrections and angelic interventions are required. I do this primarily in my devotions, rather than a street corner, but the point is, I'm manipulating the script to align with the will of God, my heart's desires, and the blessing of God I see on my life. It not only changes my expectations, but it changes the future as well. I'm not just a deluded optimist, I'm a King with a dream and enough of a warrior to reel it in—so are you. Get your sword; we have some gates to crash.

Here's the best Christmas gift you can have—your heart's desire. Kings have the privilege of asking for and receiving everything they need to make those desires a reality. It's true, "there is no Santa Claus." But, the dream doesn't end there. There is a God in heaven that has declared us to be His friends and delights in granting requests to Kings. He's invited us into His plan—the beauty, the adventure, the intimacy, the power, the grace, and the meaning.

Of all the things across which I've stumbled in this amazing journey toward releasing Kings, there is one revelation that is most liberating. God's scheme was to create me in His image with His heart so that He now freely can grant "my" heart's desire. My will is His will (thanks to Him), and we're on the same team. It's wonderful!

> *At that time you won't need to ask me for anything, for you can go directly to the Father and ask him, and he will give you what you ask for because you use my name. You haven't tried this before, [but begin now]. Ask, using my name, and you will receive, and your cup of joy will overflow.*
>
> (John 16:23–24 TLB)

Knowing that God is helping us keep the dream alive through trials is the foundation to keep right on asking, the topic of the next chapter.

CHAPTER 14
YOU HAVE TO ASK

God is moving Kings from a place of feeling rejected (by both men and God) to a place of feeling chosen. One of the great ways God is moving men and women from the discard pile to the starting line-up is through answered prayer.

One camp is receiving, or about to receive, great breakthroughs and they know it. Another camp is too discouraged to pray and their heart sounds like Habakkuk.

> *How long, O LORD, must I call for help, but you do not listen?*
>
> *Or cry out to you, "Violence!" but you do not save?*
>
> *Why do you make me look at injustice? Why do you tolerate wrong?*
>
> *Destruction and violence are before me; there is strife, and conflict abounds.*
>
> *Therefore the law is paralyzed, and justice never prevails.*
>
> *The wicked hem in the righteous, so that justice is perverted.*
>
> (Habakkuk 1: 2–4)

Here is the Lord's answer in the very next verse, and we can sense it in our hearts for this hour.

> *Look at the nations and watch—and be utterly amazed. For I am going to do something in your days*

that you would not believe, even if you were told....
(Habakkuk 1:5)

Another sign—Although I'm prone to miss the little things that God does to remind us that He is faithful, I'm trying to get better at watching for His cues. One weekend our youngest son, Ben (20), was home. We're "empty nesters" so it's always good to have kids show up. He stayed awake all night to leave for a cattle roundup at 3:00 a.m. We got home late in the afternoon and he took a nap. I went in to wake him . . . really for no good reason. I noticed sweat on his forehead while he was sleeping and I just watched him for a moment. The area above his brow was sprinkled with tiny, sparkling, golden specs. My first thought was that he must be wearing some kind of new make-up about which he wasn't telling me. My second thought was that it had rubbed off from some girl he was dating. The third thought (we're not all that speedy around here) was that it was an angelic "dusting" and that the Lord was showing me another sign. Ben's a marketing major in college. The next morning I went in again to wake him (and check for the gold dust). This time all was normal, so when he awoke, I shared what I'd seen the afternoon before and simply prayed—declaring God's prosperity, generosity, and ministry on his life. But, I fully am expecting to be utterly amazed by the goodness of God in Ben's Life.

It's Here! When we Kings take the time to prophetically hear the voice of God, we move from Habakkuk 1: 2–4 to verse 5. Now, the consequence of being aware of the magnitude of God's plan, His choosing and election on our lives, the open door to prosperity, and the opportunity to convert money into ministry, is all pretty exciting. Even if our ship hasn't come in (literally), I'm still seeing something in the Spirit that my heart can't deny, and I can't help but be excited . . . and I experience another verse from Habakkuk:

. . . Yet I will wait patiently. . . . Though the fig tree does not bud and there are no grapes on the vines, though the olive crop fails and the fields produce no food, though there are no sheep in the pen and no cattle in

the stalls, yet I will rejoice in the LORD, I will be joyful in God my Savior.

(Habakkuk 3:16–18)

Why joy on the inside when there is no answer on the outside? Faith doesn't just believe in the sense of mental alignment. The substance of faith is the prophetic assurance that the answer is there. We possess the "substance" of something that is about to materialize, and we have "evidence" of something we can't see (Hebrews 11:1). It thrills our hearts and gives us a logical and spiritual basis to keep on asking. I have to discipline myself to "ask," because the reality of the nearness of the answer is so close it feels as if it's already here.

> *Ask and it will be given to you; seek and you will find; knock and the door will be opened to you. For everyone who asks receives; he who seeks finds; and to him who knocks, the door will be opened. Which of you, if his son asks for bread, will give him a stone? Or if he asks for a fish, will give him a snake? If you, then, though you are evil, know how to give good gifts to your children, how much more will your Father in heaven give good gifts to those who ask him!*

(Matthew 7: 7–11)

. . . **so ask!** Ask for your heart's desire, and, ask for the manifestation of what God already has shown that belongs to you.

And, if you've already asked, ask again. We have not because we ask not. Now that you know that and you're not afraid to keep on asking, there is one more ingredient to ignite your passion. You have to try, the topic of our next chapter.

CHAPTER 15
YOU HAVE TO TRY

What stops you from succeeding is revealed with this simple question, "What makes it OK for you to not even try?"

I give up! We've all heard sermons about "letting go and letting God." Surrender has been a big theme. The message we often take home is that if we're really spiritual, God will intervene on our behalf, work behind the scenes, and make good things happen that don't depend on our intellect or effort. If we think of our intellect and effort as coming from a sinful heart that can't produce anything good, then a successful surrender is the best scenario for which we can hope. Wave the white flag and wait for a miracle.

I want to suggest that our hearts and minds are places where God writes His plan. This is one of the great promises of regeneration that God is powerful enough to accomplish.

> *This is the covenant I will make with the house of Is-rael after that time, declares the Lord. I will put my laws **in their minds** and **write them on their hearts**. I will be their God, and they will be my people.*
> (Hebrews 8:10) [Emp. added]

> *I will give you a new heart and put a new spirit in you; I will remove from you your heart of stone and give you a heart of flesh. And **I will put my Spirit in you** and move you to follow my decrees and be careful to keep my laws.*
> (Ezekiel 36:26–27) [Emp. added]

Having a dream, realizing it's from God (after a little discernment), and giving yourself permission to pursue it, is the starting place for experiencing the life of Christ. So, the first questions are, "Do you have a dream?" and "What is it?" Many Kings have an answer for those questions, but still lack a plan. Let's go on to the next step.

I've found most people do have a dream. Actually, the Holy Spirit has written on all of our hearts, so, theologically, we all have a dream or a desire. Most of us recognize it as being from God. The second step is "trying." A dream or a desire never gets from theory to practice until we try. Dreams remain promises until we try to make them reality. I want to replace some of the "surrender" in your relationship to God with "trying." Here's what will happen.

Trying means asking, seeking, and knocking—Willingness to try something God puts into your heart conveys your confidence in His leadership. He wants you to take the initiative to pursue your heart's desire. We're so trapped in worrying about failure (and sin) that we often never give God's leading a real "try." If you try, the door will open!

> So I say to you: Ask and it will be given to you; seek and you will find; knock and the door will be opened to you. For everyone who asks receives; he who seeks finds; and to him who knocks, the door will be opened. Which of you fathers, if your son asks for a fish, will give him a snake instead? Or if he asks for an egg, will give him a scorpion? If you then, though you are evil, know how to give good gifts to your children, how much more will your Father in heaven give the Holy Spirit to those who ask him!
>
> (Luke 11: 9–13)

Some 30, some 60, and some 100 fold—In the parable of the sower (Matthew 13) the seed is "the message about the Kingdom." This promise of seeing your heart's desire fulfilled is a central part of that Kingdom message. The man who hears the word and understands it produces a crop because he "tries" (AKA "obeys").

> *. . . But the one who received the seed that fell on good soil is the man who hears the word and understands it. He produces a crop, yielding a hundred, sixty or thirty times what was sown.*
>
> (Matthew 13:23)

Joshua—Remember all those exhortations to "be strong and courageous." God was telling Joshua to try. Fear causes us to freeze and withdraw from the battle. Fear of presumption has frozen many out of the will and blessing of God. Having the confidence to expand your corner of the Kingdom means two things; you're going to try, and you're going to face some resistance from the enemy. You may experience an occasional failure and require a few resurrections. It's part of entering the fray—you'll live and not die. Your discernment will sharpen and wisdom will grow.

> *. . . for though a righteous man falls seven times, he rises again. . . .* (Proverbs 24:16)

> *Blessed is the man whom God corrects; so do not despise the discipline of the Almighty. For he wounds, but he also binds up; he injures, but his hands also heal. From six calamities he will rescue you; in seven no harm will befall you.*
>
> (Job 5:17–19)

> *A righteous man may have many troubles, but the LORD delivers him from them all; he protects all his bones, not one of them will be broken.*
>
> (Psalm 34:19–20)

> *If the LORD delights in a man's way, he makes his steps firm; though he stumble, he will not fall, for the LORD upholds him with his hand.*
>
> (Psalm 37:23–24)

Making disciples who try—I'm really grateful to God and my parents for putting me in an environment to try things. In hindsight, they were small town things . . . 4H horses and basketball. But they were huge to me. It didn't matter that is was a small district in a small state. Getting picked for that all-conference team, winning a championship, riding the winning horse at the fair . . . forever etched the concept of "going for it" in my heart. Once tasted, that thrill of success overrides my fear of failure. When our four kids were growing up, I watched for opportunities to encourage them to excel in something they enjoyed.

Go for it. On our trip to the Netherlands, my first stop was to spend time with Cees Bakker. He's a wonderful Dutch brother, friend, and a tireless organizer of our trips there. I was a little concerned about how our message would be received. He spoke something that I later realized was very prophetic. He said, "John, you may as well go for it." God echoed that phrase in my heart every time we ministered. I tried to release my heart to the greatest degree possible. It was the first time I'd consciously given myself that level of permission to go out on a limb in expression, in the prophetic, in every way I could. Cees' words set my heart free. I set my heart free on hearing them. Regardless of what we do, I hear the voice of God saying the same thing to Kings around the world in this hour. Go for it with gusto . . . with all your heart.

> *Love the Lord your God with **all your heart** and with all your soul and with all your strength and with all your mind.* (Luke 10:27) [Emp. added]

> *Whatever you do, work at it **with all your heart**, as working for the Lord, not for men.* (Colossians 3:22–23) [Emp. added]

Are you convinced that God has authored desires in your heart? Can you imagine the excitement of a dream come true? The next section is all about your purposes—becoming more intentional about the desires of our hearts.

KEY II
I'M PASSIONATE—
FOLLOWING THE DESIRES OF MY HEART
EXERCISES AND QUESTIONS

Remember when you were young? Dreaming and playing was second nature. Then it seemed we had to grow up, get serious, go to work, earn a living. It's not easy to release your heart, live your dream, and conquer all the responsibilities and opportunities of life.

1. Are you comfortable with your emotions? What would need to happen to get you really excited?

2. On a scale of one to ten, with 10 being totally confident . . . How much do you know your hearts desires, trust your heart, and act on your passion? Examples please.

3. What hidden dreams have you given-up on or buried? What if God said, It's my absolute will and desire for you to pursue, find, and live those dreams?

4. If God's will is hidden or somehow intertwined with the desires of your heart, which desires are synonymous with His will?

5. How would you feel, what would you think about, and what would you do today, if one of your own heart's desires were your assignment from God?

6. If an angel showed up with a message from God saying whatever you do would totally succeed, but you could only have one focus, what would you choose?

7. Setting money and current job aside, what would you really like to do with your life? What would it look like in the middle of your dream come true—say in five years?

   a. Describe your dream home _____

   b. Car_____

    c. Office_____

    d. Family_____

    e. What would people be thanking you for?_____

KEY III
I'M PURPOSEFUL—BRIDGING MY DESIRES AND GOD'S PLAN

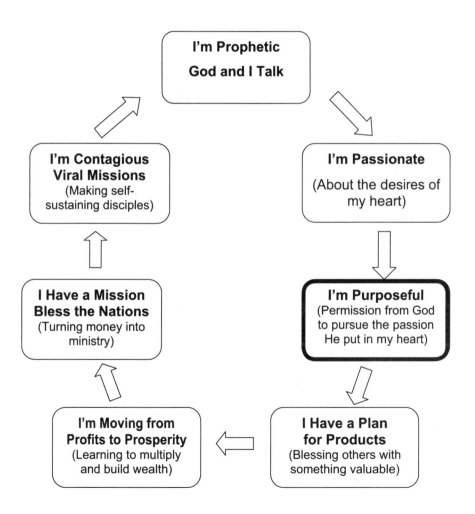

I'm Prophetic
God and I Talk

I'm Contagious
Viral Missions
(Making self-sustaining disciples)

I'm Passionate
(About the desires of my heart)

I Have a Mission
Bless the Nations
(Turning money into ministry)

I'm Purposeful
(Permission from God to pursue the passion He put in my heart)

I'm Moving from
Profits to Prosperity
(Learning to multiply and build wealth)

I Have a Plan
for Products
(Blessing others with something valuable)

T his is the stage where we gradually become more "purposeful" about implementing the dreams in our hearts about which we're passionate. We start to feel God's permission to try to assemble the puzzle pieces of a vision that actually will start a great adventure. We approach decision-making and guidance with more purpose, and we start taking ownership of our destiny. Instead of waiting to see God do it all, we begin to walk toward it.

Your next move—We stop viewing the obstacles to assess the degree of waiting required. Instead, we move on to a view of life that focuses on the next move I make. No more victim mentality!

Risk—You're created in God's image. He's written His plan and purpose right into your DNA. You naturally gravitate toward the gifts and callings for which you are designed. God values initiative so much that His term for Christians without it is "wicked."

Make the decision. Now you're ready to make a decision, instead of depending on God to make it for you. Use wisdom, the experience of friends, a mentor, and networking with other Kings. Be practical!

Out of the boat—Initiative starts with a word, "ask." Nearly everything Jesus did in the New Testament was in response to a request.

A cause—Passion means you've found something you enjoy doing—it's exciting. Purpose means you've applied that passion to a cause. You see your goals as part of a larger scheme that the Holy Spirit is orchestrating throughout the earth. You're an important player on a much bigger team.

Goals are spiritual. Formalize your goals into a list on which you can focus in prayer, and change as you go. The reason? Articulating your heart's desire is the process that releases creativity and innovation. Breakthroughs, ideas, opportunities, and innovations come to people with goals. It's a tangible expression of your faith.

Innovation—Creativity is a godly process that anyone can learn. It starts with an idea that gets translated into words (goals) and spoken into existence by faith (with work and enough persistence to finish).

Chapter 16
What's Your Next Move?

The question from God—I really enjoy meeting Kings and hearing their stories. John Laney is a developer in a very prophetic package. He's working in our city, so I have lunch with him quite often. Last week, as we were eating, he looked across the table and said, "John, what's your next move?" Normally I'm full of plans and ideas to walk through doors the Lord is opening. But as I listened to my own answer, I was convicted by how "lame" it sounded. Here's what I said:

The answer—I have two categories of goals. One is to be a King. I personally want to experience prosperity and generosity (or ministry) at a much greater level. *Knowing* the theory and *implementing* it are two different things. We've made investments that have started to materialize in a small way, and we're "waiting" on God for them to increase greatly. In the mean time, I'm working away as an engineer (same as the last 30 years).

My second goal is to communicate the message in *Releasing Kings* to help others find a personal release in their destinies. I love to turn the lights on for people who haven't really found the adventure of their ministry callings. We do this through books, a weekly e-mail newsletter, training materials on our web site, and conferences as far away as the Netherlands. I get a steady stream of inquiries and I have invitations. But, again, I'm "waiting" on God for some of those things to materialize.

Waiting on God—Now, as I listened to my answer to John's question ("What's your next move?"), it dawned on me that the answers I gave for the two areas closest to my heart centered around waiting for God to do something. As I verbalized my "waiting theology," John sat politely eating his lunch and said nothing—while the

Holy Spirit began to "eat my lunch." Here's what I heard the Lord say:

"John, you're not waiting on me, I'm waiting on you. I already have opened doors. It's time for you to walk through them. I'm waiting on your initiative. What is your next move?"

Adjusting my approach to God—Right now God is maturing Kings from being servants who follow Him to friends who share His vision and ministry. As a servant, my theology was to avoid presumption and to stay in perfect alignment with the leading of the Holy Spirit. My worship songs, preaching, and life aligned around that approach to God . . . "following." Now the Lord is saying, "Walk with me, not behind me." Not everyone is ready for that level of relationship. That's OK because I believe we mature spiritually by being good servants who first learn to follow well. Many who are called to be Kings are finding that "serving" eventually runs its course and dries up. God begins to relate to us as friends, Kings, and co-laborers, and He starts waiting for us to show some leadership.

> *Enoch walked with God 300 years and had other sons and daughters. Altogether, Enoch lived 365 years.* ***Enoch walked with God****; then he was no more, because God took him away.*
>
> (Genesis 5:22–24) [Emp. added]

> *Noah was a righteous man, blameless among the people of his time, and he* ***walked with God****.*
>
> (Genesis 6:9) [Emp. added]

> *I no longer call you servants, because a servant does not know his master's business. Instead,* ***I have called you friends****, for everything that I learned from my Father I have made known to you. You did not choose me, but I chose you and appointed you to go and bear fruit—fruit that will last. Then the Father will give you whatever you ask in my name.*
>
> (John 15:15–16) [Emp. added]

*And God raised us up with Christ and **seated us with***
***him** in the heavenly realms in Christ Jesus, . . .*
(Ephesians 2:6 NIV) [Emp. added]

The transition I want to share the emotions of making this transition from waiting on God to walking with Him. When you get near the end of your "servant" mentality, several things happen.

1. Yearning for more—First, you will start yearning for something more than serving in another man's vision. Along with the yearning, you'll be sorting through feelings of guilt for doing or thinking what you used to call rebellion (it's really condemnation). God is activating your heart's desires (something servants aren't allowed).

2. Making decisions—Next, you won't get guidance on everything about which you pray. The Lord is trying to teach you to make decisions on your own that align with His will, instead of making all of them for you.

3. Who's waiting on whom? Lastly, you'll view it all as a wilderness test and wait for God's rescue—which doesn't come. You will be waiting on promises which feel delayed, and at some level you may start nursing a little grudge that God isn't responding to your prayer, that His answer seems too late, that His presence is too distant. If you try to remain merely a faithful servant, your little grudge is likely to turn into a mountain of resentment.

Your first wobbly steps as a King—Most of us can identify with the transition. Many are now walking with God in some brand new ways and finding the adventure that was supposed to be part of their destinies all along. Here's what they are experiencing and doing.

1. Write down the next steps. In your quiet time, prayerfully ask the Lord to walk with you into your "next steps" and start writing them down. No more condemnation. It's not about you. It's about expanding the Kingdom. If you feel unworthy, get over it. God wants to bless the nations, and He's stuck blessing His people and granting their hearts' desires to get the job done (actually it's

His plan to work through us and He loves it). So be blessed—its God's will for you. You just have to figure out how, not whether.

2. Pray with authority. Prophetically declare your next steps with authority, and begin to act with the expectation of success. God wants to make your name great! You won't let Him if you're stuck in false humility at "servant."

3. God loves you. Before you can go to Step 4, you have to pass this test. God wants to bless you because He loves you. He's so abundant, so generous, and such a great Father that He just enjoys blessing His kids. Some things He'll do for you have no other purpose than to express His love. Don't deflect that love and blessing. Learn to bask in it. Be thankful for it and enjoy it. For me "it" is our kids and their spouses, the grandkids, horses, and ranching.

4. Ministry—Make the connection between your blessing and your ministry. God is blessing you in order to bless others. My goal is prosperity at a level where I can give 90% and live on 10%. I, and many others, are sponsoring the next reformation where Kings call forth their dreams, change the world, and have fun doing it. At this level, He will speak with you face to face.

> *I will make you into a great nation and I will bless you; I will make your name great, and you will be a blessing. I will bless those who bless you, and whoever curses you I will curse; and all peoples on earth will be blessed through you.* (Genesis 12: 2–3)

> *With him will I speak mouth to mouth, even apparently, and not in dark speeches; and the similitude of the LORD shall he behold. . . .*
> (Numbers 12:8 KJV)

Bottom line—Being entrepreneurial, creative, and innovative really reflects the nature of God. You were created in His image and destined to walk with Him. Make the transition and see what treasures are already in heaven with your name on them. You've been authorized to bring them to earth.

I will give you the keys of the kingdom of heaven; and whatever you bind on earth shall have been bound in heaven, and whatever you loose on earth shall have been loosed in heaven.

(Matthew 16:19 NASU)

Truly I say to you, whatever you bind on earth shall have been bound in heaven; and whatever you loose on earth shall have been loosed in heaven. Again I say to you, that if two of you agree on earth about anything that they may ask, it shall be done for them by my Father who is in heaven. For where two or three have gathered together in My name, I am there in their midst.

(Matthew 18:18–20 NASU)

Are you ready to make a move? There is always some risk involved but there is a way to safely navigate the alligators . . . as we'll discuss in the next chapter.

CHAPTER 17
TAKE INITIATIVE AND RISK

All the Kings I've met have a single ingredient in common: they are creative and take the initiative and risk to pursue their dreams. It's no accident that they have a different play book. Most of us have come from a theological framework where initiative and rebellion were closely related. Spirit-filled Christians didn't make a move without the leading of the Holy Spirit. Even though we believed every-minute-guidance was Scriptural, it was a little disappointing to find out how little guidance we actually received, compared with our theological expectations. Let's review the verses we used to zero out our initiative.

The Son can do nothing by Himself. This verse seems plain enough. If Jesus can do nothing by Himself, we certainly shouldn't either.

> *Jesus gave them this answer: "I tell you the truth, the Son can do nothing by himself; he can do only what he sees his Father doing, because whatever the Father does the Son also does.*
>
> (John 5:19)

Please look at this passage in context. Jesus isn't just a robot responding to the Father's signals. The Father shows Him all He does. Secondly, Jesus is allowed to give life to whomever He pleases. Thirdly, the Father entrusts "all judgment" to the Son. In reality, Jesus has lots of room and responsibility for personal initiative. He chooses to remain in fellowship with the Father, but He's not in the position of waiting for direction before He can make a move. He's got the general plan, the Father's heart, and an occasional midcourse correction.

> *For the Father loves the Son and shows him all he does. Yes, to your amazement he will show him even greater things than these. For just as the Father raises the dead and gives them life, even so the Son gives life to whom he is pleased to give it. Moreover, the Father judges no one, but has entrusted all judgment to the Son, ...*
>
> (John 5:20–22)

By myself I can do nothing. We often interpret this phrase as a prohibition against independent thought and action. In reality, Jesus is not pointing to a "sergeant/private" relationship where He's merely carrying out orders. Jesus is pointing to the relational proximity between Himself and the Father.

> *By myself I can do nothing; I judge only as I hear, and my judgment is just, for I seek not to please myself but him who sent me.*
>
> (John 5:29–30)

I do nothing on my own. In this passage Jesus is explaining His Sonship with the Father. His point is not to emphasize limits on His initiative, but to explain that His actions and words have roots in the Father. Jesus is explaining His divinity.

> *So Jesus said, "When you have lifted up the Son of Man, then you will know that I am [the one I claim to be] and that I do nothing on my own but speak just what the Father has taught me."*
>
> (John 8:28)

Apart from me you can do nothing. In the following passage Jesus is explaining that we are connected relationally to a larger source of life and a larger plan of action. However, that fact doesn't diminish the need for our initiative within our own callings or spheres of influence. Notice this passage ends with the promise, "ask whatever you wish." An amazing degree of freedom, when you think about it. In fact, it's a mandate for initiative.

I am the vine; you are the branches. If a man remains in me and I in him, he will bear much fruit; apart from me you can do nothing. If anyone does not remain in me, he is like a branch that is thrown away and withers; such branches are picked up, thrown into the fire and burned. If you remain in me and my words remain in you, **ask whatever you wish, and it will be given you.**

(John 15: 5–7) [Emp. added]

The zero initiative scenario—When we emphasize our sinful nature and the problems we have with initiative, rebellion, presumption, etc., we seem to be left with a message that we shouldn't take any initiative. After hearing those verses and the testimonies of others hearing from God for everything, we start to imagine that we can't hear from God because He isn't showing us when and where and how to take every step.

Here's the biblical reality. God does speak to us; He does treasure our relationship with Him and our awareness of His plans and purpose. The Holy Spirit can lead us specifically and prophetically at times. But most of the time He doesn't spell out all the details. We're left to make decisions and take risks—period. If you think you're alone in this, you're not. Even people who claim constant guidance in every area are stretching the truth, based on their understanding of correct theology. In fact, every spiritual person I know has gone through seasons of not being able to hear from God at all. God often waits to see what kind of initiative our hearts will invent.

Remember how the LORD your God led you all the way in the desert these forty years, to humble you and to test you in order to know what was in your heart, whether or not you would keep his commands.

(Deuteronomy 8:2)

Here's the test: How close to the heart of God is your heart when the heavens become brass and your communication with God is difficult? It should be so close that we naturally desire God's plan even when He withdraws His immediate presence. That's the wilderness test. He puts His will into our hearts so that we don't need constant promptings about every detail. He's making sons, not robots.

> *"This is the covenant I will make with the house of Is-*
> *rael after that time," declares the* LORD. *"I will put my*
> *law in their minds and write it on their hearts. I will*
> *be their God, and they will be my people.*
>
> (Jeremiah 31:33)

> *"This is the covenant I will make with them after that*
> *time," says the Lord. "I will put my laws in their hearts,*
> *and I will write them on their minds."*
>
> (Hebrews 10:16)

Give yourself permission to take a risk. Here's why! You're created in God's image. He's written His plan and purpose right into your DNA. You naturally gravitate toward the gifts and callings for which you are designed. When I take initiative that leads to failure, I fail right into the arms of a loving Father who treasures my initiative. He wants His kids to be responsible and creative. God doesn't fall off the throne when we fail. In fact, He has the power to turn "all things" to good (Romans 8:28).

The ten minas—Jesus told a parable of a King giving each of his ten servants money to invest in his absence. This parable is relevant because He invests in each of us exactly the same way.

> *A man of noble birth went to a distant country to*
> *have himself appointed king and then to return.*
> *So he called ten of his servants and gave them ten*
> *minas.. "Put this money to work,' he said, 'until I*
> *come back.'"* (Luke 19:12–13)

The results came in as follows.

> *"The first one came and said, 'Sir, your mina has*
> *earned ten more.'*

'Well done, my good servant!' his master replied. 'Because you have been trustworthy in a very small matter, take charge of ten cities.'

The second came and said, 'Sir, your mina has earned five more.'

His master answered, 'You take charge of five cities.'

Then another servant came and said, 'Sir, here is your mina; I have kept it laid away in a piece of cloth. I was afraid of you, because you are a hard man. You take out what you did not put in and reap what you did not sow.' "   (Luke 19:16–21)

This King left no other instruction than to put his money to work. Our instruction is also fairly general: "Go into all the world and make disciples." Now, if you're expecting guidance for every detail according to a faulty theology, you simply are positioning yourself to bury your mina and get in a lot of trouble. Now remember seven of the ten didn't even show up to give an account. Verse 27 is apparently the Kings attitude toward them.

" '. . . But those enemies of mine who did not want me to be king over them—bring them here and kill them in front of me.' "   (Luke 19:26–27)

What about the servant who was too afraid to take any initiative or risk his mina?

His master replied, "I will judge you by your own words, you wicked servant! You knew, did you, that I am a hard man, taking out what I did not put in, and reaping what I did not sow? Why then didn't you put my money on deposit, so that when I came back, I could have collected it with interest?" Then he said to those standing by, "Take his mina away from him and give it to the one who has ten minas."

(Luke 19:22–24)

93

Bottom line—God values initiative so much that His term for Christians without it is "wicked." Taking action and risk is part of following Jesus, especially for Kings. You've been given the stewardship of your time, talents, vocation, and money. Your job is to take that one mina and increase it 30, 60, or 100-fold. God will guide you in a way that will require you to take initiative and risk. You won't get every detail spelled out . . . and, frankly, doing nothing is probably worse than making a mistake. God blesses people who pray and dream and imagine and move on their heart's desire. The more they move the more guidance they get. God is inviting you to pursue your hearts' desires. Abundant life is waiting for your initiative. It's worth the risk because you're destined to succeed. God is for you. And besides all that, it's fun!

Feeling a little more entrepreneurial? We hope so. One of my personal ambitions is to help Christians connect with a Kingly anointing. Try reading the interviews we've posted on the web (www.releasing-kings.com/Interviewing-Kings.html). They all are inspiring and some of those folks would be glad to help you get started if you find an area that "fits" you. Here's a quote for Kings that I really love from C. Thomas Anderson:

> What is the perfect will of God? In short, it is these four things. Get saved. Live right. Build wealth. Build the Kingdom. This is where God wants to lead us.

Can you feel God leading us to take the next step and make some entrepreneurial decisions? You can minimize the risk by using wisdom, the experience of friends, finding a mentor with experience, and networking with other Kings. How to make those decisions is the topic of our next chapter.

CHAPTER 18
HOW TO MAKE A DECISION

Releasing Kings does a great job of helping people connect with an anointing to be spiritual, entrepreneurial, and missions-minded. Many of us are in a process of translating the "release" into concrete actions in the marketplace. Here's how one person put the question in a recent e-mail.

> I've just recently finished (consuming) *Releasing Kings* and now, am blessed by your newsletters. Both continue to draw me in, speak to my soul, and "stir the juices" . . . My question is painted with a broad stroke. When you're certain God has "poised" you for release, and you've won the battle over doubt, discouragement, and every (catastrophic) fiery dart, and you're able to stand in the knowledge and confidence of what He has promised (Hosea 2:14–23)—how do you "take the initiative" to step out (even when you so want to) to be a King, when that "step" is not made clear, through you or by the Lord?

Hearing God—Many are tweaking the way they hear from God. Let's try to distinguish the two approaches.

1. The classic, traditional approach is centered on a belief that "sovereignty" means that God knows and controls the future. Under this view our only job is to find the singular "will of God" and do it. Initiative is viewed as a swamp of presumptuous shipwrecks fraught with temptations that play on our carnality. We only move when the Spirit leads.

2. The Kingly approach is premised on the fact that God has reserved a portion of the future for us to rule and reign with him. "God's sovereignty" is understood to mean that He can do anything He wants and intervene at anytime He wants. However, He chooses to let much of history unfold through the activity of Kings. Thus, our initiative plays a huge role in co-laboring with Christ and releasing God's power to change our world. Since we're created in His image, we consider the desires of our hearts as holy ground—deserving attention, discernment, and action. The Promised Land is a place where our heart's desires, our gifts, our vocations, and our ministries all align with God's plan for our lives, a plan in which we play some role in defining via our "relationship" with Jesus.

From a practical standpoint, all Christians face weighty decisions without absolutely clear guidance on what to do. The classic approach (item 1 above) actually causes well-meaning believers to invent hunches and impressions and act on them, as though they came from the Holy Spirit. They are theologically unable to accept that their hearts' desires and initiative may be the means through which God expects them to make decisions. The other reality is our history. We all can point to initiatives we entertained that failed utterly and obviously were not the "path of the righteous."

Mentoring—There is a common missing ingredient that will facilitate our transition from (1) to (2). It's wisdom, the practical guidance of someone with experience. I believe God is unfolding a fathering ingredient for marketplace ministries that fits this apostolic age. Instead of (or in addition to) closeting ourselves in prayer and fasting, waiting for that perfectly clear guidance, let's define a direction based on the desires of our hearts and find a believer who has the background to help us make it happen. Really successful Kings love to share their secrets with people who share their hearts' desires.

Have a father and be one—Said another way, we see Christian friends in this transition waiting on God to deploy their hearts' desires. Let's help them. Some are in their 20's and 30's and others are boomers nearing retirement.

Instead of watching them flounder through all the blind alleys, help them define a path (or better yet, several paths) through the forest that they can implement with a little guidance. Help them connect the dots between their own hearts' desires, gifts, ministries, and vocations. Make people development a part of your own marketplace ministry.

Networking—I'm amazed at the level of networking between Kings already operating in their anointings. It's one of the biggest things Kings do that others don't. Their breakthroughs come in the form of divine appointments with other people. One friend (John Laney) is particularly fun to watch. Every time he hears about someone on a related track, he picks up the phone and introduces himself, trolling for divine appointments. He treats every new acquaintance as though he or she may be an angel sent by the Lord to help him or join him in building the Kingdom. He expects divine contacts and facilitates them. His mentor operates at funding levels one or two orders of magnitude above John's. But, there is no doubt in my mind that John will surpass the level of blessing on his mentors because of his initiative, faith, favor, and business plan. Why does he have such blessed mentoring? Initiative—he picked up the phone, had the lunch, and walked through the open door. More specifically, he found a way to help his mentor, built a relationship, gained the experience, and "earned" the favor.

Ready to make those decisions? The first step in getting out of the boat is asking God for your dream, the topic of the next chapter.

CHAPTER 19
WHY STEP OUT OF THE BOAT?

Why Kings are different—They are enterprising, creative, fruitful, prosperous, and totally excited about expanding the Kingdom of God to bless the rest of the world. They are not just businessmen; Duane Smith is a realtor who put together a community crusade and conference attended by 800 pastors in India. Duane was inspired by another "engineer" friend of his (Howard Ferris) who spends his vacations doing evangelistic crusades which he personally funds and organizes. The latest was in Pakistan. *"More than 55,000 participated in the historical healing crusade and approximately 20,000–25,000 turned their lives towards God." That's a quote from the local Pakistani newspaper! Think about it! An engineer said "why not" and went and did it.*

    "Come" and join the party. I can't resist trying to package their anointing for the rest of us. Why do they step out of the boat and others stay in? Why do some venture into the marketplace while others retain refuge inside the Church? Why are we prone to find sanctuary inside the sanctuary?

> *"Lord, if it's you," Peter replied, "tell me to come to you on the water." **"Come," he said.** Then Peter got down out of the boat, walked on the water and came toward Jesus. But when he saw the wind, he was afraid and, beginning to sink, cried out, "Lord, save me!" Immediately Jesus reached out his hand and caught him. "You of little faith," he said, "why did you doubt?"*
>
> (Matthew 14:28–31 NIV) [Emp. added]

Let's Roll. Todd Beamer's phrase echoed in our hearts after the 9/11 crash in Pennsylvania. He symbolized in one heroic act the key ingredient of people who make a difference in the Kingdom; they do something. Some are willing to take initiative. Peter's walk on the water didn't really start with Jesus; it started with a desire in Peter. He asked the Lord to tell him to come. In fact, as we read the New Testament, most of what Jesus did was in response to a request. Most of us (especially Spirit-filled Christians) have a theology that requires God to take the initiative before we act. We are proud of our humility, ability to obey, sensitivity to the Holy Spirit, and our servant status. However, Kings just aren't that way. Right or wrong, they are out there doing things. And you know what: God is multiplying their impact in the marketplace and putting His favor on them.

Aside—A few years ago I would have led the pack in refuting the above paragraph with regard to the evils of lone rangers, presumption, independent spirits, rebellion, etc. No longer—I've met too many people in the marketplace who are making it happen. I've seen the favor of God on their lives. I'm hungry for the same thing. And, as the word is getting out that God is releasing Kings, there is now beginning a jail break of reformational proportions.

Start Asking—Here's a principle throughout Scripture that we may have missed. God is searching for a love relationship with people who are willing to make a decision and ask for their own hearts' desires . . . not for some brash, selfish request; they are more mature than that. But, they do move an occasional mountain or conduct an occasional crusade. They initiate the request in confidence because they know they were created in God's image; that He's placed His own desires in their hearts. They view themselves as Kings; friends of God who share the Lord's burden for our cities and nations.

> *Ask and it will be given to you; seek and you will find; knock and the door will be opened to you. For everyone who asks receives; he who seeks finds; and to him who knocks, the door will be opened.*
>
> (Matthew 7: 7–8)

If you, then, though you are evil, know how to give good gifts to your children, how much more will your Father in heaven give good gifts to those who ask him!
(Matthew 7:11–12)

Again, I tell you that if two of you on earth agree about anything you ask for, it will be done for you by my Father in heaven. For where two or three come together in my name, there am I with them.
(Matthew 18:19–20)

" 'If you can'?" said Jesus. "Everything is possible for him who believes." Immediately the boy's father exclaimed, "I do believe; help me overcome my unbelief!"
(Mark 9:23–24)

... Therefore I tell you, whatever you ask for in prayer, believe that you have received it, and it will be yours. And when you stand praying, if you hold anything against anyone, forgive him, so that your Father in heaven may forgive you your sins.
(Mark 11:24–25)

I tell you the truth, anyone who has faith in me will do what I have been doing. He will do even greater things than these, because I am going to the Father. And I will do whatever you ask in my name, so that the Son may bring glory to the Father. You may ask me for anything in my name, and I will do it.
(John 14:12–14)

If you abide in me, and my words abide in you, you will ask what you desire, and it shall be done for you. By this my Father is glorified, that you bear much fruit; so you will be my disciples.
(John 15: 7–8 NKJV) (See also Psalm 91)

I tell you the truth, my Father will give you whatever you ask in my name. Until now you have not asked for anything in my name. Ask and you will receive, and your joy will be complete.

(John 16:23–24)

Yet you do not have because you do not ask. You ask and do not receive, because you ask amiss, that you may spend it on your pleasures.

(James 4: 2–3 NKJV)

Dear friends, if our hearts do not condemn us, we have confidence before God and receive from him anything we ask, because we obey his commands and do what pleases him.

(I John 3:21–22

This is the confidence we have in approaching God: that if we ask anything according to his will, he hears us. And if we know that he hears us—whatever we ask-we know that we have what we asked of him.

(I John 5:14–15)

Ask big. We serve a big God with a big task to build the Kingdom, and He's looking for people with big hearts. Go ye.

Becoming purposeful means you're not afraid to ask. Now that you have asked, let's take the next step. Purpose also means you've applied your passion to a cause that is bigger than yourself. You see your goals as part of a larger scheme that the Holy Spirit is orchestrating throughout the earth. You're an important player on a much bigger team. More in the next chapter.

CHAPTER 20
KINGS HAVE A CAUSE

"Purpose driven life" has been a prophetic theme over the last couple of years. Rick Warren hit a vein of God's Spirit that has been echoing in the hearts of God's people. Most of us have taken spiritual-gift inventories and discovered something about what motivates us and what we enjoy doing. Each of us is a package of unique history, natural talents, spiritual gifts, ministries, passions, and purpose.

I want to emphasize the importance of finding your life's cause or purpose. Let's look at the seven gifts listed in Romans 12.

> *We have different gifts, according to the grace given us. If a man's gift is **prophesying**, let him use it in proportion to his faith. If it is **serving**, let him serve; if it is **teaching**, let him teach; if it is **encouraging**, let him encourage; if it is **contributing** to the needs of others, let him give generously; if it is **leadership**, let him govern diligently; if it is **showing mercy**, let him do it cheerfully.*
> (Romans 12: 6–8) [Emp added]

Kings can come in many different gift mixes. Those in the financial world are motivated to make money and to be generous. Having your life "cause" clarified will give meaning and direction to your passions and gifts. What happens if we haven't connected with our cause?

Teachers—Imagine a teacher, motivated to study and get in front of people and share information. How do they appear with no cause? Their heart isn't in their teaching. It lacks direction, passion, and substance. They start to sound similar to some of the boring college professors you had in school.

Leaders—Imagine a leader without a purpose. He would be motivated to direct the lives of others but wouldn't have a direction to point them. With no purpose, they are considered autocratic. With God's purpose, they are considered as prophetic servants. Big difference!

Kings—in the business realm are motivated naturally to make money. It's a gift that ignites some of their passion. Now if that package is connected to a cause and people can see the fruit of their prosperity they rejoice. If no cause or purpose is visible, then Kings commonly are considered greedy, selfish, or imbalanced. That is probably a legitimate criticism of the "faith movement." There is just too little emphasis on the cause behind the wealth.

Passion for prosperity—The Bible has a consistent theme that supports a theology of prosperity for Kings. A good example is in Proverbs 8. Those who believe wealth is evil quote verses 17 and 19. Those who can see prosperity in Scripture quote verses 18 and 21. I personally like all five verses; Kings seeking God, finding wealth, and bearing the fruit of a generous lifestyle.

> *I love those who love me, and those who seek me find me.*
>
> *With me are riches and honor, enduring wealth and prosperity.*
>
> *My fruit is better than fine gold; what I yield surpasses choice silver.*
>
> *I walk in the way of righteousness, along the paths of justice, bestowing wealth on those who love me and making their treasuries full.*
>
> (Proverbs 8:17–21)

Balance—Wealth is a necessary tool that Kings use to fulfill their destinies. When they seek God, they find Him—and His wealth. They also find the purpose behind the wealth. Kings have an anointing to convert wealth into ministry and make a huge difference in society and missions. Doors are being opened for you to connect wealth and ministry.

Vision and cause—Vision is a picture of your life's purpose or cause in the future. We can live for a vision, but we'll die for a cause when we're connected to something here and now. A vision can excite you, but a cause gives you power (1) to get wealth, and (2) to convert it to ministry that expands the Kingdom. Do you feel your heart's desire or "cause" is being disregarded by God? Don't give up! Your flesh may be tired, or the enemy may want to steal your inheritance, or God may want to test your mettle. Nurture your heart's desire instead of giving up on it.

> *Why do you say, O Jacob, and complain, O Israel, "My way is hidden from the LORD; my cause is disregarded by my God"? Do you not know? Have you not heard? The LORD is the everlasting God, the Creator of the ends of the earth. He will not grow tired or weary, and his understanding no one can fathom. He gives strength to the weary and increases the power of the weak. Even youths grow tired and weary, and young men stumble and fall; but those who hope in the LORD will renew their strength. They will soar on wings like eagles; they will run and not grow weary, they will walk and not be faint.*
> (Isaiah 40:27–31) [Emp. Added]

Times and seasons—Right now the Holy Spirit is connecting Kings to their tools (one is wealth) and their cause or purpose in life (which expands the Kingdom). We use the following graphic in conferences to depict this process: (1) we network opportunities for Kings to overflow their cups, then (2) we help them find opportunities to be a blessing and carry out the great commission.

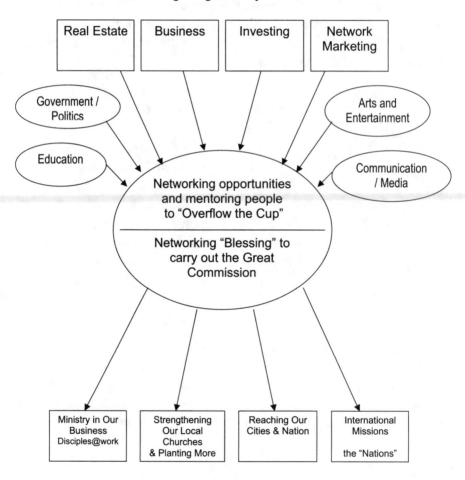

Networking Kings—Why We're Here!

| Real Estate | Business | Investing | Network Marketing |

Government / Politics

Education

Arts and Entertainment

Communication / Media

Networking opportunities and mentoring people to "Overflow the Cup"

Networking "Blessing" to carry out the Great Commission

| Ministry in Our Business Disciples@work | Strengthening Our Local Churches & Planting More | Reaching Our Cities & Nation | International Missions the "Nations" |

Kings—Making Money to Make a Difference

74

CHAPTER 21
GOALS ARE SPIRITUAL

Why have goals? Only a few percent of people have a journal with written goals which they update daily (or at least several times a week). Some view goals as an expression of selfish carnality. Others worry about being too "driven." Goals orient our faith and enable God to grant our desires; we become and receive that about which we think most of the time. On the down side, if our focus is primarily on our fears (fear of failure; fear of what others think), we tend to inherit those fears. Our "faith" actually can work against us.

> *For the thing which I greatly feared is come upon me, and that which I was afraid of is come unto me.*
> (Job 3:25 KJV)

> *What the wicked dreads will overtake him; what the righteous desire will be granted.*
> (Proverbs 10:24)

Unintentional goals—We all have goals, whether or not they are written and intentional. In fact, our current lives are the unforgiving product of the goals we've set through the present time. No goals equal no life. "Faith" operates by intentionally focusing on a desire or request and asking for it; then walking toward it with the actions that will produce it. Seeing answered prayer (fulfilled goals) is a great source of spiritual "life" and "joy."

> *Hope deferred makes the heart sick, but **a longing fulfilled is a tree of life**.*
> (Proverbs 13:12) [Emp. Added]

> *I tell you the truth, my Father will give you whatever you ask in my name. Until now you have not asked for anything in my name. Ask and you will receive, and **your joy will be complete**.*
> (John 16:23–24) [Emp. Added]

I like myself! Having goals requires an admission that your life has value (to God, for example). The essence of willingness to set goals answers a single question that many people avoid: "What do I really want to do with my life?" I want to suggest that even God is asking each one of us that question. To answer correctly you have to place a value on your ability to make a contribution. I believe we each have value for several reasons: (1) we were created in God's image, (2) He loves us and puts value on our relationship, and (3) He has a plan in which we've been invited to participate. We get to choose from works that were created with us in mind.

> *For we are God's workmanship, created in Christ Jesus to do good works, which God prepared in advance for us to do.* (Ephesians 2:10)

Add all that up and you should be able to look into a mirror and say with a straight face, "I like myself." You can't really export something you don't have. Do you want others to feel loved? You have to feel that way first! Want to help them be happy? You have to be happy first. The Bible doesn't really tell us to "love ourselves." It assumes we already do.

> *The entire law is summed up in a single command: "Love your neighbor as yourself."*
> (Galatians 5:14 see also Leviticus 19:18, 34)

The idea that your job is to serve and make others happy while being unhappy yourself may be good for monks, but not for Christians. Your life was intended to be a cup that is continually overflowing in every area; a well that waters others from its own abundance.

Being intentional about goals—Passivity is the cancer of faith. No one was more intentional than our greatest biblical examples . . . David, Jesus, Paul. Their determination and persistence in the face of adversity are a testimony of their faith.

> God *"will give to each person according to what he has done." To those who **by persistence** in doing good seek glory, honor and immortality, he will give eternal life.* (Romans 2: 5–7) [Emp. added]

Excuses—The greatest hindrance that keeps us from our destinies in God are the beliefs that make it OK to not even try. Here are a few that need a proper burial.

I can't

> *I can do all things through Christ who strengthens me.* (Philippians 4:13 NKJV)

I've tried—seven times seventy?

> *Those who hope in the* LORD *will renew their strength. They will soar on wings like eagles; they will run and not grow weary, they will walk and not be faint.* (Isaiah 40:31)

I'm too old/I'm too young/I'm a woman—Great, you're perfect.

> *And afterward, I will pour out my Spirit on all people. Your sons and daughters will prophesy, your old men will dream dreams, your young men will see visions. Even on my servants, both men and women, I will pour out my Spirit in those days.* (Joel 2:28–29)

I'm not qualified—Welcome to the club! No one else is either.

> *Not that we are competent in ourselves to claim anything for ourselves, but our competence comes from God.* (II Corinthians 3:5)

> *But we have this treasure in jars of clay to show that this all-surpassing power is from God and not from us.* (II Corinthians 4:7)

How to set goals—In each of the five steps (below), I've listed some of my own entries in each category as examples. Take the time to make your list and incorporate it into your devotions and prayer journal. These are your hearts' desires and assignments from God. They're important.

First—list your values. Make a list of your highest values (virtues, priorities, etc.). What is most important in every area of your life?

1. God—a communicating relationship

2. Sue—a communicating, romantic relationship

3. Releasing Kings message

4. Wealth conversion to missions (be a King)

5. Kids and grandkids

6. Horses, ranching

Second—trash your obstacles. Make a list of the things standing in the way of achieving those values. As a separate exercise, list ten ways to overcome each obstacle. Again, here are mine.

1. Distraction of job, time consumption

2. Investment returns delayed

3. Resolution of ranch

4. Lack of focus on releasing Kings

Third—life time goals—List your lifetime goals. What do you want to do with your life?

1. Life's path—Example and teach others to live abundantly and bless the nations.

2. Finances—Millionaire investments, business starts, ranch-

ing. Show abundance and generosity by example. Live on 10%. Teach my natural and spiritual children to do the same.

3. Organize an army that changes the world's nations/cultures with the gospel of abundance, creativity, and resurrection life.

4. For people who got lost on the way; pastor them to their dream; include them in the cause.

5. Deploy an army of like-minded mentors and coaches to help with #4.

6. Walk with Sue as she grows in her unique gifting.

Fourth—3–6 month goals—List your more immediate goals that can be achieved in the next three to six months.

1. Outline, draft, and edit the next book that helps translate vision to practice.

2. Conduct three releasing Kings conferences and make them available as CD's and downloadable MP3 files. Include Sue in two of them.

3. Develop a conference around the theme of the new book.

4. Develop an on-line training course, live conference calls, recorded archives downloadable on the Internet. Add a "store" to the website—get help!

5. Develop a means to network Kings so they can find one another for investments, business opportunities, missions, and microbusiness.

6. Multiply the ministry of releasing Kings—release the message through others; find a way to involve those called to participate. Network Kings with coaches and advisors.

Fifth—get help. Share some of your more important goals with someone and ask for help reaching them. "Help" could be in the form of mentoring/advice, or it could be someone who jumps in and adds something to the equation because it aligns with one of his/her own goals. Significant achievements always involve the help of others.

Adjust your goals often. God will speak to you about the above four lists nearly every day. So . . . change them every day. They are a living prayer list and a focal point for your faith and actions. Lastly, do something every day toward fulfilling your goals. Remember, we over estimate what we can do in a month and underestimate what we can do in ten years. Get started. You're much better off making a mistake or a poor decision and correcting it than doing nothing.

Take it easy with your prophetic language . . . "God told me, showed me, gave me." Leave God and yourself room to adjust your plan. No one sees or plans perfectly, partly because all the outside variables keep changing. Our decisions are made in the absence of perfect information about the future. We mature rather slowly in our ability to make good decisions, in case you haven't noticed! I read a statistic that suggested about 70% of our decisions are "wrong"—meaning they need some post-decision adjustments to stay on track. Even God makes midcourse corrections!

> *For now we see through a glass, darkly; but then face to face: now I know in part; but then shall I know even as also I am known. . . .*
>
> (I Corinthians 13:12 KJV)

Use the process above to formalize your goals into a list on which you can focus in prayer, and change it as you go. The reason? Articulating your heart's desire is the process that releases creativity and innovation. Breakthroughs, ideas, opportunities, and innovations come to people with goals. It's a tangible expression of your faith. More about creativity in the next chapter.

CHAPTER 22
CREATIVITY—FROM IDEA TO REALITY

I'm fascinated by the creative process and have been asking Bob Bartow for an interview for months. He is an artist with a business called "Creative Images" - a rare combination of creative genius and King. You'll enjoy his interview and his graphic arts. They often are sold at prophetic conferences and through his web site. His process is simple—the Lord shows him a prophetic image, he gets a digital camera, takes the picture, brings it home to his computer, and "doctors it up" until it's reality. Pretty simple! Actually, it is simple, and you can learn the process yourself quite easily and apply it in your own life.

1. Get the picture Everything that ever has been created and every innovation started with an idea. You have to picture something in your mind that you want to have happen. Call it imagination, revelation, meditation, or dreaming . . . you have to see it first. Some people get hindered at this point, waiting for God to show them something or tell them something. Most prophetic people allow themselves only one avenue, "God showed me." That's great if He does, but if you don't happen to be from that stream, it may feel more as if you birthed the idea. That's OK and here's why.

> *Now faith is the **substance of things hoped for**, the evidence of things not seen.*
> (Hebrews 11:1 KJV) [Emp.added]

God can work through the desires of our hearts. He usually does. The idea that He prophetically drops something about which we've never heard is actually the exception, and it's often just theological semantics. If we think of ourselves as inherently sinful, we view our hearts as "desperately wicked," and we don't expect our personal hopes and goals to be worthwhile. Actually, they are very worthwhile in God's mind, and He defines faith as the substance of things "hoped for." So, the creative process can start with the list of things for which you hope. Pretty exciting, isn't it? It's Christmas all year long for Kings!

2. Put it in words. In the beginning "God created." How is fairly straightforward, "And God said, let there be light." Since you're created in His image, and He's invited you into the creative process, it's worth following His example. Translating your idea or dream into words is the next step in creating something new. Notice that, even for God, it's not the last step. He had to separate the light from the darkness; some amount of work here because it took a day, and the whole process took six days and then He rested. You're not done just because you get it into words but, it's a very important step. Notice that God calls things that are not as though they were; and Abraham (father of the faith) believed in hope as a key part of his "becoming."

> As it is written: "I have made you a father of many nations." He is our father in the sight of God, in whom he believed — the God who gives life to the dead and **calls things that are not as though they were.** Against all hope, **Abraham in hope believed and so became** the father of many nations. . . .
>
> (Romans 4:17–18) [Emp. Added]

This part of the process also can include writing the words down, making goals out of them, and prophetically declaring them. Prophetic declarations have the power of prayer and angels start lining up the universe to make reality line up with your petition. Count on miraculous intervention; just don't substitute it for "work"—the next step.

Note: At this stage there are all kinds of counterfeits in the new age movement and in humanistic psychology that leave God out of this process. One author I read actually believed the material world only exists in our imagination, so it wasn't too surprising that changing his thoughts changed his reality. I hope he gets saved before he finds out the truth after it's too late. My point is this. Don't allow abuses of the truth to keep you from it.

3. Get to work. We demonstrate our faith by our works. Those ideas and words finally are translated to business plans and reality by the things we do. We often feel this part of the process isn't very spiritual, when it's really the greatest expression of faith. By faith, Noah built an ark. It cost money and took lots of sweat and time to build. He got his hands dirty (had fun) and took some heat from the neighbors. This is a masculine stage. We get to bring something into the material world in the confidence of our faith. We know it not only originated in the hope of our hearts' desires. We also know it's very much in God's heart and will. After a strenuous day, we can lie back and sense the blessing of God and the cheer of the heavenly host on our lives. It feels good to work.

4. Finish. Normally, in the course of the above three steps, you'll encounter several levels of warfare. Ideas and words usually get hit with unbelief and discouragement. When you get to the work stage, you may encounter all kinds of tiring and demotivating obstacles. The stereotype of spirituality is that nothing ever goes wrong. Saying that "everything always goes wrong" isn't true either; but, sometimes it feels that way. Real spiritual maturity will finish. It's not usually easy, but it is "easily possible."

We probably should add "resurrection" as another category. People who have learned to "finish" usually have learned to survive things such as bankruptcy and other kinds of setbacks. Prophetic insight and intercession can save us from many of these obstacles, but it's really your faith that enables you to turn "lemons into lemonade" and will get you through. So, suck it up and have an exploit for breakfast!

> *And we know that **all things work together for good** to them that love God, to them who are the called ac-*

cording to his purpose.
(Romans 8:28 KJV) [Emp. added]

*but the people that do know their God **shall be strong, and do exploits**.*
(Daniel 11:32 KJV) [Emp. added]

. . . but the people who know their God will display strength and take action.
(Daniel 11:33 NASU)

Gitter' done: It's a jailbreak out there and we're about to have a big party. When you've created something, God will show you the next thing, and your horizons, your heart, your ministry and your finances will expand with each new passion made real.

Now that you have a glimpse into the creative process, the next step is to build a plan around your unique idea that expresses your passion. We also want a product that will produce a profit . . . the topic of the next section.

KEY III
I'M PURPOSEFUL—
BRIDGING MY DESIRES AND GOD'S PLAN
QUESTIONS AND EXERCISES

This isn't school, or homework, God wants your life work and ministry to be fun! It is possible to engage your heart, enjoy your passion, and impact the world. If we believe it, it's time to do something with it. This is the time to be daring. Let's pretend we're Alexander Graham Bell in the process of inventing the telephone, or Thomas Edison inventing the light bulb. It takes risk, initiative, and a path forward.

1. Find a friend and ask this question, "What's your dream and how can I help you make it happen?" Listen carefully and help them any way you can.

2. Identify two people you know who would give you practical help in stepping into your dream. Share your dream and solicit their input. Write down their reaction.

3. Pretend you're going to get your dream off the runway in the next 15 months. What needs to happen specifically in these next six months to get started?

4. What's holding you back? Make a list of every obstacle, person, or fear. Now list five ways to get around each one.

5. It's easier to give excuses to why something won't work, than to take responsibility for directing your life. Do you act like God blesses your Kingly initiative, or are you theologically stuck? What "belief" is holding you back.

6. "Reflective Creation" process. . . . Choose to create and connect your faith to your action!

KEY IV
I HAVE A PLAN FOR PRODUCTS—
ADDING VALUE TO THE LIVES OF
OTHERS (MINISTRY)

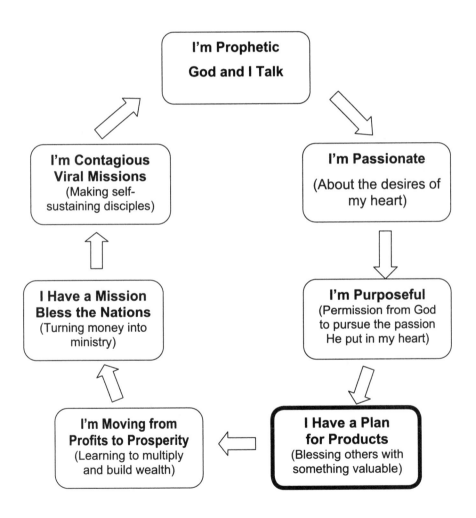

E xtending our goals and creativity to a product that will produce a profit is what allows us to give ourselves to the ministry
aspect of our passion. We produce something that has value and
blesses others. We've outlined the five ingredients in planning for
a profit. They are summarized below and discussed in the chapters
that follow.

Be positive. Having a plan entails being positive about success-
fully implementing it. We have to manage our thoughts, words, and
actions to represent the focus of our faith.

Expect opportunities. The Lord is bringing a steady stream of
opportunities to those who have eyes to see them. Set your expectations, persistence, and networking accordingly.

Expect warfare. Goal number one is to separate Christians
from their dream. Your hearts' desires are the seed bed of faith and
the vehicle for God's will in your life. Proverbs calls your heart a
wellspring of life. If the enemy can discourage you from "trying" it's
an obvious defeat and your "well of hope" will go dry.

Plan your inheritance. God has plans to prosper us and give us
the Kingdom as part of our inheritance. Our job is to plan around
the desires of our hearts. What we think, say, and do play big roles
in our ability to receive.

Plan your exploits. Modern-day exploits with Kings have an
entrepreneurial ingredient. They accept abundance as a fact of "life
in Christ," and they believe and work to see it manifested. They enjoy the creative process, and they are finding open doors to celebrity
and wealth, which they view as tools of ministry—to make others
successful.

Plan a product. One of your first spiritual assignments as a
King is to make money. Your passion will lead you to a product or a
service and then to a profit. When it does, your ministry will begin.
Until then, your entire ministry is a spare-time activity.

CHAPTER 23
POSITIVE MENTAL ATTITUDE

PMA Larry King recently hosted a news interview on CNN with six guests—all motivational speakers promising health, wealth, and anything else if you get on the right frequency. Some even made vague references to God, while others mentioned cosmic energy. I'm attracted to that stuff as a moth to a flame so I got the transcript off the internet and read it carefully. At the end, they recommended the very best resource in the field (a movie).

The bad news Before watching or ordering the movie, I did a little more homework and found it was really an infomercial to sell more materials, and that one of the creators channels in her new age seminars . . . great promises but all leading to a spiritual dead end. The reason God is so opposed to dabbling in false spirituality is that it's similar to a gateway drug that leads to even greater deception. He finds it detestable because it leads people away from a real relationship with Jesus. Vibrations, crystals, and cosmic forces just don't substitute for knowing Jesus.

> *Let no one be found among you who sacrifices his son or daughter in the fire, who practices divination or sorcery, interprets omens, engages in witchcraft, or casts spells, or who is a medium or spiritist or who consults the dead. Anyone who does these things is detestable to the LORD, and because of these detestable practices the LORD your God will drive out those nations before you. You must be blameless before the LORD your God.*
>
> (Deuteronomy 18:10–13)

The good news The good news is that the things Larry's PMA guests were promising are exceeded greatly by what is already available to you and me as Christians.

> *You will make known to me the path of life; In your presence is fullness of joy; In Your right hand there are pleasures forever.*
>
> (Psalm 16:11 NASU)

The PMA message resonates with people right now because God is saying something very similar throughout the land. He's activating your heart's desire to accomplish His purposes. In some ways, that's a radical departure from our evangelical focus on the sinfulness of mankind. However, it gets equal time in the Bible. Here's the balance. Sin is a reality for all of us that is solved only through Jesus' forgiveness via the cross. God, however, doesn't stop at forgiveness of sin. He writes His laws on our hearts and grants our desires as a means of building the Kingdom. Honestly, most Christians think it's too good to be true and don't operate in all that Jesus provided for us.

> *You have granted him the desire of his heart and have not withheld the request of his lips.*
>
> (Psalm 21:2)

> *Delight yourself in the LORD and he will give you the desires of your heart.*
>
> (Psalm 37:4)

> *He fulfills the desires of those who fear him; he hears their cry and saves them.*
>
> (Psalm 145:19)

> *Praise the LORD, O my soul, and forget not all his benefits—who forgives all your sins and heals all your diseases, who redeems your life from the pit and crowns you with love and compassion, who satisfies your desires with good things so that your youth is renewed*

like the eagle's.   (Psalm 103: 2–5)

Ask whatsoever . . . John 14:13–14; 15:7–8; 15:16; 16:22–24; I John 5:14–15; I Kings 3:5.

Here are four practical steps to reach the same level of maturity that Kings use all the time to see their hearts' desires come to fruition. In Proverbs 4:23 we are told to guard our hearts or thoughts because our actions will follow our attitudes; verse 24 says to use your words to say what God says—be positive; verse 25 tells us to keep our eyes on the prize—stay focused on our vision; verse 26 says to do the things that make our vision come to pass—expect success.

> *Above all else, **guard your heart**, for it is the wellspring of life.*
>
> *Put away perversity from **your mouth**; keep corrupt talk far from your lips.*
>
> *Let your eyes **look straight ahead**, fix your gaze directly before you.*
>
> *Make **level paths for your feet** and take only ways that are firm.*
>   (Proverbs 4:23–26) [Emp. added]

1. **Manage your thoughts** with devotions to set your heart and mind. Most Christians are concentrating on what they *don't* want to happen, and if you asked them to define clearly what they would like to see happen, they couldn't articulate it (let alone have faith for it). For every bad thing that does happen, most of us have a system of blame already established that keeps us from taking the positive steps to reverse or resurrect the situation.

Write down the desire of your heart. Answer God's question, "What would you have me do for you?" Get your vision for your life on paper, then make it a matter for prayer. If we believe God wants to grant the desires of our hearts, we surely must be specific. Use our interview format as a template. (See www.releasing-kings.com/Interviewing-Kings.html)

In the morning write down seven things you would like to see happen consistent with your dream. Make the list, pray through it, and do it every day during your morning devotions.

In the evening review the list and see how many answers you received and what progress you made. Make those items topics for praise and thanksgiving.

2. Manage your words. Most of us just naturally articulate negative expectations over positive ones at a ratio of about five to one. Allow the Holy Spirit to correct your negativity and set your words to prophesy your dream into existence. Say what God says about you, your situation, and other people. Your words prophesy your future. Spend them as money . . . wisely on your vision, instead of your fears.

> . . . Abraham. He is the father of us all. As it is written: "I have made you a father of many nations." He is our father in the sight of God, in whom he believed—the God who gives life to the dead and **calls things that are not as though they were.**
>
> (Romans 4:16–17) [Emp. added]

> I tell you the truth, if you have faith as small as a mustard seed, **you can say to this mountain,** "Move from here to there" and it will move. Nothing will be impossible for you.
>
> (Matthew 17:20) [Emp. added]

3. Keep your eyes on the prize. You can have all the cars, houses, and boats you want because God is abundantly generous. You need enough of that "stuff" to convince you that God really is extravagant in His love for His kids. But, the prize is ministry. Your real satisfaction comes from converting the overflow from a full cup to ministry that blesses the nations and blesses the Lord.

> . . . all peoples on earth will be blessed through you.
>
> (Genesis 12:3)

4. Set your actions toward your dream. Take the initiative with your actions to walk toward your dream. That's how God designed this army of "friends" to work. Do what it takes to make the vision a reality, starting now. Take the seven things for each day's devotions and put feet on them. If you can't find something to do to make progress that day, at least make it a matter of intercession. Be tenacious!

> *Moses my servant is dead. Now then, you and all these people, get ready to cross the Jordan River into the land I am about to give to them—to the Israelites.* **I will give you every place where you set your foot,** *as I promised Moses.*
> (Joshua 1: 2–3) [Emp. added]

Whenever I hear myself or others say: "I'm waiting for God's timing," or "I've set out a fleece," or "I'm waiting for God to open a door," one thought comes to mind . . . "What pabulum! Why are we making all these excuses?" What can we do today? Put your foot on some land! This army is all about exploits, not excuses.

> *Today, if you hear his voice. . . .*
> (Psalm 95:7) [Emp. added]

> *So, as the Holy Spirit says:* **Today,** *if you hear his voice. . . .* (Hebrews 3:7) [Emp. added]

> *Today, if you hear his voice. . . .*
> (Hebrews 3:15) [Emp. added]

> *Therefore God again set a certain day, calling it* **today. . . .**
> (Hebrews 4: 6–7) [Emp. added]

When your attitude is consistently positive and focused on the good things of God, something very interesting happens; opportunity knocks. You will begin to see the doors God has open for you.

> *Finally, brothers, whatever is true, whatever is noble, whatever is right, whatever is pure, whatever is lovely, whatever is admirable—if anything is excellent or praiseworthy—**think about such things**.*
>
>   (Philippians 4:8) [Emp. added]

CHAPTER 24
OPPORTUNITY IS KNOCKING

*. . . For everyone who asks receives; he who seeks finds; and to **him who knocks**, the door will be opened.*
(Luke 11: 9–10 NIV) [Emp. added]

Here I am! I stand at the door and knock. If anyone hears my voice and opens the door, I will come in and eat with him, and he with me.
(Revelation 3:20)

We've just had a few cool nights and you can tell those crisp, colorful fall days are right around the corner. In the same way, we can sense a season changing in the Spirit. Kings are being given new opportunities, and our hearts must be awakened to hear God knocking on our individual doors. How can we be sure we hear the knock?

*And of the children of Issachar, which were men that had **understanding of the times**, to know what Israel ought to do. . . .*
(I Chronicles 12:32 KJV) [Emp. added]

*I slept but **my heart was awake**. Listen! My lover is knocking. . . .*
(Song of Solomon 5:2) [Emp. added]

Why Kings see opportunity—Most of us can point to some time in our lives where we've missed a great opportunity. Here's a story that illustrates the way we "miss."

127

A man got caught in his home during a flood, and it became an island in the midst of the ever-rising current. A neighbor saw him and extended a branch and said, "Grab hold and I'll pull you to safety." The man replied, "The Lord will save me." The water rose past the first floor and another neighbor came with a boat and offered a ride to safety. The man said, "The Lord will rescue me." Finally the water rose so high the man was sitting on his roof when a helicopter came by and threw down a rescue ladder. The man's reply was the same. The water continued to rise until the house and the man washed away and he drowned. When the man got to heaven he was somewhat indignant and asked the Lord why He didn't rescue him. God said, "I offered to rescue you three times and you turned me down."

Creative or entrepreneurial believers see things that others don't. They really are different in several areas. The good news is that you can make adjustments in those areas and learn to "see" your opportunities, as well.

Expectations—Healthy Christians expect good things from God. They view themselves as friends of God instead of sinful servants. They see God as relational and caring, instead of a mysterious force whose will is somehow behind every disaster that occurs. They see the future as bright and share a determination to make it that way. In short, they have been given great opportunities in the past, and they expect them to continue in the future.

They knock. Poverty stresses the importance of humility, and waiting, and is overly fearful of presumption. God has given us a different Spirit that knows how to multiply; a Spirit of power, and of love, and a sound mind. If these folks don't hear God knocking on their doors, they just knock on His. When the door opens, they find a Father who just loves kids who seek Him with their whole hearts. He loves kids who knock, and ask, and seek.

*For this reason I remind you to fan into flame the gift
of God, which is in you through the laying on of my
hands. For **God did not give us a spirit of timidity**,
but a spirit of power, of love and of self-discipline.*
(II Timothy 1: 6–7) [Emp. added]

They network. The last trademark of poverty is independence.
As the man who drowned, they wait for God to show them something unique, something for them alone. If you could interview
Kings with wealth, you would find "work" and "network" to be key
ingredients. Their stories involve networking with other creative
entrepreneurs who showed them an opportunity, and they jumped
on it. They acted . . . worked . . . responded. When the knock came,
they opened the door. It's so easy it feels as if it's cheating. They accepted a "gift." But then, isn't that how we got saved? Isn't that how
God does everything? He gives a gift, but we have to accept it and
use it.

Opportunity is knocking for all of us. The Holy Spirit is knocking on our doors; inviting us to new adventures and new levels of
blessing and new levels of ministry to others. It's prudent at this
stage to be aware that the enemy would like to discourage us away
from our heart's desire. We need to know how to handle a little
warfare.

CHAPTER 25
NOT-SO-SPIRITUAL WARFARE

Bumps in the road—"Spiritual warfare" brings up images of angels and demons flying in formation through the heavens and engaging in World-War-I style dogfights. I certainly don't discount unseen warfare; at times it does feel as if we're a little ignorant of devices. As entrepreneurs pursue their dreams of expanding the Kingdom, they should expect to be targeted and understand a little more about enemy tactics . . . without attributing more attention, power, and stature to the enemy than they should. His main weapon is deception. It's really tough to stay demon-possessed these days; the number of Spirit-filled Christians who understand their authority in Christian nations is wonderful. Some of the greatest strongholds yet to be broken are more akin to ideologies, philosophies, and false religions.

> . . . *in order that Satan might not outwit us. For we are not unaware of his schemes.*
>
> (II Corinthians 2:11)

> *See to it that no one takes you captive through hollow and deceptive philosophy, which depends on human tradition and the basic principles of this world rather than on Christ.*
>
> (Colossians 2:8)

Is spiritual warfare real? Yes, it certainly is and it's much closer to home than you may realize. Here's how and why.

The primary strategy—The enemy's goal number one against you isn't quite as dramatic as the movies suggest. It is simply to separate Christians from their dreams. Your heart's desire is the seed bed of faith and the vehicle for God's will in your life. Proverbs calls your heart a wellspring of life. If the enemy can discourage you from "trying," it's an obvious defeat and your "well of hope" will go dry.

> *Above all else, guard your heart, for it is the wellspring of life.* (Proverbs 4:23)

Identity—Another related battlefront is our personal identity. Many Christians retain a vague sense of unworthiness. They believe the lie that they are primarily sinners, and that nothing good will come *from them* or *to them*. When something bad happens, they simply accept it . . . no resistance, no appeals; defeats satisfy a hidden expectation that we somehow deserve it.

Kings carry themselves in higher esteem. They understand that obstacles to their personal actions are really affronts to the "King of Kings," and they won't tolerate them. I really was blessed this week by an e-mail of a friend who encountered resistance in a business deal that could cost him dearly. He met with the person threatening the extortion to try and reconcile the problem. Good so far? What was different is that he brought his lawyer and fully was prepared to serve the "problem" with formal legal action in the event he wouldn't reconcile. Many would turn the other cheek to the devil and lose, then try to find a Bible verse to justify it. Thank God for Christians with a backbone.

> *And from the days of John the Baptist until now the kingdom of heaven suffereth violence, and the violent take it by force.* (Matthew 11:12 KJV)

> *So he made a whip out of cords, and drove all from the temple area, both sheep and cattle; he scattered the coins of the money changers and overturned their tables. To those who sold doves he said, "Get these out of here! How dare you turn my Father's house into a market!"* (John 2:15–16)

Any biography of great accomplishments always carries a parallel story of great obstacles and great tenacity in warfare. We shouldn't be surprised when we run into problems, and we always should be prepared to get out the pots and pans and make lemonade out of lemons. Sue and I did a conference near Jackson Hole, Wyoming, earlier in January. We made reservations and planned an extra day to see the scenery and get acquainted with the people. We were leaving early Friday morning, but the night before we left, we found a message from Delta Airlines on our answering machine; a fog rolled in and flights out of our city were cancelled Thursday through Saturday. I tried other airlines, other cities; nothing worked. So we just checked the weather report, hopped in the car, and drove ten hours. Of course, the weather was perfect, and as the sun came up on our way over, we saw the sky full of jet streams. The conference and the wonderful people we met there were worth every minute, and we actually enjoyed the drive. Don't be surprised by a few obstacles and distractions; do keep your eyes on the prize.

Finances—Since the ministry of Kings touches commerce so often, financial issues are a common battlefront. Too often we've been exposed to stories of checks arriving in the mail as miraculous provision. "Spiritual" is sometime poorly defined as putting yourself in a vulnerable position so that your faith can be exercised to draw on God's miraculous provision, absent any planning of our own. We often expect God to bail us out of problems, while God is expecting us to learn to be good stewards and multiply our talents. When business or personal finances get into trouble, it's nearly always a cash-flow issue, and cash-flow problems nearly always trace back to having no credible financial plan or strategy. Business plans are spiritual! If I don't have a financial plan or strategy, I'm "planning" to fail, and the devil will provide the anointing and the opportunity.

There is also a theological ingredient to financial failure scenarios. We often embrace a prophetic urging with a financial commitment, sometimes called "a leap." If it doesn't work, our choices are to blame God or blame ourselves. It's a little embarrassing to blame the devil, because then we have admitted our lack of power.

The "mature" answer is to take the prompting of the Holy Spirit as an indication of what God does want to do. (I find most people do have a good grasp of the general direction.) However, it's our responsibility to put a plan around that guidance and implement it in a way that works . . . we anticipate things that could go wrong and set aside the finances and schedule to cover them. If we believe God has the future all predestined and we just have to get on board, then it's logical to skip the planning, assuming God has it all under control. If the future is at least partially "open," then the plan (our plan) has to be dynamic, and our future is full of contingencies that God is expecting us to manage. If you can grasp this reality, it will save you a ton of frustration. It also will put you in a position that can be multiplied. God really is favoring Kings who are connected to their own hearts and His heart to build the Kingdom. It's fun! We're much greater than any resistance the enemy can put before us.

> *The LORD will grant that the enemies who rise up against you will be defeated before you. They will come at you from one direction but flee from you in seven.*
>
> (Deuteronomy 28:7)

> *. . . the people that do know their God shall be strong, and do exploits.*
>
> (Daniel 11:32 KJV)

> *You, dear children, are from God and have overcome them, because the one who is in you is greater than the one who is in the world.*
>
> (I John 4:4)

Did you know you have an inheritance? Your heavenly Father has some great things specifically stored up for you. It's time to understand those specifics and make a plan to inherit them.

CHAPTER 26
MAKING A PLAN FOR YOUR HERITAGE

No weapon forged against you will prevail, and you will refute every tongue that accuses you. ***This is the heritage of the servants of the LORD....***
(Isaiah 54:17) [Emp. added]

We interviewed John Laney and I've tried to capture some of the essentials of his "life message." John is a developer with a distinctly prophetic and bold gift mix.

Most Christians generally would agree that God has good things in store for them. God has a plan to prosper us, and it's a good idea to get that plan in writing and execute it now, instead of leaving it up in heaven for the millennium. If you have a plan, it will change three things:

1. The way you think (faith)

2. What you say (confession)

3. What you do in order to make the plan a reality (actions). What Christians often miss is that God expects us to participate in making the plan, instead of just waiting for it to happen.

> *... For I know the plans I have for you," declares the LORD, "**plans to prosper you** and not to harm you, plans to give you hope and a future. Then you will call upon me and come and pray to me, and I will listen to you. You will seek me and find me when you seek me with all your heart. I will be found by you," declares the LORD....* (Jeremiah 29:11–14) [Emp. added]

1. What you think—Nothing delights the Father more than seeing His kids inherit their portion of the Kingdom. That extends to granting you the desires of your heart. You reach Spiritual maturity when you and God have the same desires. It's much easier than you think. God created us in His image to have those desires, and for whatever pollution sin has brought into our lives, God has promised to give us a new heart.

> *"Do not fear, little flock, for **it is your Father's good pleasure to give you the kingdom**."*
> (Luke 12:32 KJV) [Emp. added]

> *Trust in the* LORD *and do good; dwell in the land and enjoy safe pasture. Delight yourself in the* LORD *and **he will give you the desires of your heart**.*
> (Psalm 37: 3–4) [Emp. added]

Start to believe that God wants to release your inheritance, grant the desires of your heart, and prosper you. It will change your approach to life.

2. What you say—The first ramification of really being on the same page with God is authority. Your words will have the prophetic force of God's Words; you're His kid, His representative, His ambassador. You represent Jesus in the earth right now—doing even greater works as His sons (Romans 8:14) and friends (John 15:15).

> *"Have faith in God," Jesus answered. "I tell you the truth, **if anyone says** to this mountain, 'Go, throw yourself into the sea,' and does not doubt in his heart but **believes that what he says will happen**, it will be done for him. Therefore I tell you, whatever you ask for in prayer, believe that you have received it, and it will be yours. And when you stand praying, if you hold anything against anyone, forgive him, so that your Father in heaven may forgive you your sins."*
> (Mark 11:22–25) [Emp. added]

We serve a God Who calls things that are not as though they were (Romans 4:17). We share the authority to speak "our" wills into existence. When we understand God's desire to give us the Kingdom and put His favor on our lives, then we begin to speak a new language. It sounds bold and assertive to your friends. But to Jesus, it's the sound of the Kingdom of God being established on earth through a chorus of Kings using the keys God has given them to release the provision of heaven.

> *"I will give you the keys of the kingdom of heaven; and whatever you bind on earth shall have been bound in heaven, and whatever you loose on earth shall have been loosed in heaven."*
>
> (Matthew 16:19 NASU)

3. What you do This final step is astounding! Christians who begin to believe God and dare to talk about their inheritance take an amazing step. They plan to prosper and minister and receive their visions. They start taking conscious steps toward their heritage. It's similar to a business plan. Articulate the vision of your heart's desire that maps into God's plan for you, count the cost, and start moving toward the goal. Until recently, the body of Christ has been entirely too passive in this whole process. As John Laney said in his interview:

> "All things are possible to them that believe." The reason they become possible is that people who "believe" are willing "to do" what it takes. Faith has legs.

What about resistance? If you get serious about claiming your inheritance, you'll get a "wanted poster" with your picture on the devil's bulletin board. In addition, if you move away from being passive and start to implement your plan, problems just naturally arise. One failure point is facing a problem or attack and assuming it means that God has withdrawn His favor. God is not the author of attacks against His own people. He is never the One who kills, steals, and destroys His own people.

> *If anyone does attack you, **it will not be my doing;** whoever attacks you will surrender to you. . . . no weapon forged against you will prevail, and you will refute every tongue that accuses you. **This is the heritage of the servants of the LORD.** . . .*
>
> (Isaiah 54:15,17) [Emp. added]

When God did judge Egypt, there are two important aspects of how He did it that still apply: (1) All of the ten plagues came at Moses' word, and (2) none of them touched God's people. In the same way, not only are we protected from the judgments of God, we are given a way to prosper through them, and we even may have a role in turning them on or off with our words, just as Moses did. It's our heritage to defeat problems.

Questions God is asking—What's the vision of your heart's desire? What would you like to be doing in five years? How do you plan to make it happen? How will you finance it? With whom will you work?

Be assured, there is a plan specifically for you, and you'll play a big role in defining the details. It's your privilege and responsibility to begin to ask those questions, fill in some of the blanks, and implement the answers.

> *It is the glory of God to conceal a matter; to search out a matter is the glory of kings.*
>
> (Proverbs 25:2)

Once you understand something about your inheritance from God "and" you build a plan to obtain that inheritance, something amazing happens. God multiplies our relative mundane "employment" all the way up to "exploits."

CHAPTER 27
PLANNING YOUR EXPLOITS

Our tradition—There is a new sound in the Kingdom and Kings are beginning to experience a new kind of breakthrough. It's financial! Our prior model for outreach ministry (or missions) has been centered around Jesus' instructions to the disciples in Matthew 10; healing, resurrection, and deliverance. The Scripture, "The worker is worthy of his keep" is understood classically to mean that the missionary is supported by offerings. Thus, our missionaries come home regularly to "itinerate" and raise support through offerings in local churches. Traveling ministries depend on the frequency and size of offerings to survive.

> *Heal the sick, raise the dead, cleanse those who have leprosy, drive out demons. Freely you have received, freely give. Do not take along any gold or silver or copper in your belts; take no bag for the journey, or extra tunic, or sandals or a staff; for the worker is worth his keep.* (Matthew 10:8–10)

Multiplying finances—The "church-sponsored" missionary is not a bad model—it's just not the only model. What is happening in marketplace ministry is that Kings are going out with the same anointing for miracles, plus a financial ingredient. We featured an interview with Howard Ferris, a great example of an engineer with a self-supporting evangelistic gift. We are starting to see testimonies of financial breakthrough, and we're starting to disciple an anointing for finances to go with ministry.

> *Isaac planted crops in that land and the same year reaped a hundredfold, because the LORD blessed him. The man became rich, and his wealth continued to*

grow until he became very wealthy. He had so many
flocks and herds and servants that the Philistines en-
vied him. (Genesis 26:12–14)

But so that we may not offend them, go to the lake and
throw out your line. Take the first fish you catch; open
its mouth and you will find a four-drachma coin.
(Matthew 17:27)

The new paradigm—A number of changes are occurring in the Kingdom to complement a new entrepreneurial spirit. Testimonies of financial increase are beginning to come in. We're celebrating marketplace breakthroughs that used to be viewed as materialistic carnality. Now we understand that money can be converted to ministry. Our testimonies used to be "spiritual miracles" that verified that your offering would be put to good use. Now we see an anointing for signs and wonders, coupled with the financial resources to carry out ministry.

And you, be ye fruitful, and multiply; bring forth
abundantly in the earth, and multiply therein.
(Genesis 9:7 KJV)

Entrepreneurial disciples—God is putting a creative, entrepreneurial ingredient into Christians who excel in the marketplace. They accept abundance as a fact of "life in Christ," and they believe and work to see it manifested. They enjoy the creative process, and they are finding open doors to celebrity and wealth, which they view as tools of ministry to make others successful.

I will make you into a great nation and I will bless
you; I will make your name great, and you will be a
blessing. I will bless those who bless you, and whoever
curses you I will curse; and all peoples on earth will be
blessed through you." (Genesis 12: 2–3)

Sowing for increase—Instead of waiting for God's sovereignty to rain down provisions or taking the offering route, these Kings are sowing generously so they can reap generously. They are starting businesses or making investments that will result in ministry. They aggressively are pursuing God's provision in practical ways. They don't feel greedy or materialistic to the slightest degree. In fact, they find the whole process of inheriting God's abundance an exciting adventure.

> *Remember this: Whoever sows sparingly will also reap sparingly, and whoever sows generously will also reap generously.* (II Corinthians 9:6)

> *You will be made rich in every way so that you can be generous on every occasion, and through us your generosity will result in thanksgiving to God.* (II Corinthians 9:11)

Could it be me? Absolutely! Ministering out of a cup that is overflowing is what it's all about . . . Jesus paved that way to "greater works" and the abundant life that makes it possible. You'll be amazed at what you can do for God when you give yourself permission to act and take the responsibility and initiative to make it happen.

> *Freely you have received, freely give. . . .* (Matthew 10:8)

> *. . . the people that do know their God shall be strong, and do exploits.* (Daniel 11:32 KJV)

What's the next Step? Plan a product; something with such great value to others that they will "fund" your ministry in the marketplace . . . they will "buy it."

CHAPTER 28
PLAN A VALUABLE PRODUCT

Making money—One of your first spiritual assignments as a King is to make money. Here's the simple reason that I learned from my 13 years as a pastor. Ministry costs money—nothing happens without money. If you're living paycheck-to-paycheck, it's likely that you don't have a ministry. If your business or investments are overflowing, then you will be on the lookout to bless people and convert some of that money to ministry. It even frees your own time to minister in your own community, or to take missions trips.

Identify your product. When you've finished identifying the desires of your heart, your passion, your purpose, and your goals, something golden will appear . . . your ministry. You have great value to God. Remember the hidden treasure and the pearl? That's you. What you desire in your heart also has great value, not only to God but to others. Artists don't just paint for themselves. Great musicians don't play in soundproof rooms. Politicians don't give speeches in a vacuum. We "give" our gifts to bless others . . . to bless the nations.

Now, before we get too spiritual, how many paintings, concerts, and elections have you seen that are free? Get the point? What we have to give has value to God and to people. It's entirely appropriate to exchange money for that value. One of the largest strongholds of the poverty mentality is that we have no value and our vision is worthless, as well. Your passion will lead you to a product or a service, and then to a profit. When it does, your ministry will begin. Until then, your entire ministry is a spare-time activity. Your ministry and passion are important enough both to you and God to deserve your full attention. That means it has to generate a profit in order to pay the bills. "Work" in the biblically purist form, is working on your passion. That's what God designed you to do . . . so figure out a way to do it. It will bless your heart.

And if you don't labor at your passion? You'll gradually starve your passion and kill your heart. Sure, you'll still go to heaven. You just won't have any fun or fruit in the mean time.

My dad was a rancher and it was his dream. He worked hard in all kinds of weather and seldom had time for a vacation. But, every day he woke up and worked on "his" dream. He had fun doing it because the cattle, the horses, the land, and the dream were all part of his heart's desire. He passed away at 91 and left a 15,000 acre ranch to his four children—his "dream."

Don't just save, lean to sow. The first step to making money is to get out of the religious mindset of works and engage your heart. Budgets are like diets. Both are impossible to maintain over a lifetime. If you can capture your vision in goals, your natural passion will propel it to the top of your financial priority list. Buy income-generating assets that support your vision (this feels as if you're shopping!). We're not saving money for a rainy day; that just would guarantee a rain storm. We save money to spend—just change your buying habits. Instead of some "depreciating impulse item," buy yourself something that will support your vision. Start your business, buy real estate, invest in stocks, etc. That kind of spending is called "sowing" for a harvest. How should we sow (shop for our vision)? Abundantly, of course! Do you see now why your heart likes to shop? You just need to point your heart toward its first love . . . your passion.

> *Remember this: Whoever sows sparingly will also reap sparingly, and whoever sows generously will also reap generously.* (II Corinthians 9:6)

> *You will be made rich in every way so that you can be generous on every occasion. . . .* (II Corinthians 9:11)

Track your progress. We're all stewards of our time, talents, and money. As you allow your heart to go shopping for assets that align with your vision, track your progress on a personal financial statement. That is simply a one-page summary of all your assets and liabilities, summarizing your financial net worth at the bottom. You can get a free template for a financial statement at www.score.org/template_gallery.html. Your list of income-generating assets should be growing and producing more income every year throughout your life and in the end, it should be the inheritance you pass on to your grandchildren.

> *A good man leaves an inheritance for his children's children. . . .* (Proverbs 13:22)

Pick a path. As you think about your passions, ministry, and shopping for assets, the following categories may be helpful. We have interviewed Kings in each of these categories, and you can read the interviews on our web site. See www.releasing-kings.com/Interviewing-Kings.html. In addition, they are generally people who would be glad to give you some advice on how to get started.

Real estate–There is only so much land in the world and every year the price keeps going up. Rental property, raw land, and housing developments can be good opportunities.

Business—(Hard goods and services)—Starting a business in line with your passion can be very rewarding and profitable.

Internet marketing–Marketing your information over the internet is a rapidly growing field that has an affordable entry price.

Network marketing–Many network marketing companies are now internet based so you don't have to keep a garage full of product. It's an excellent place to start in business for anyone. It's also an excellent second income opportunity where you can learn vital business skills at low cost, especially selling, organizing, making presentations, accounting, team building, negotiating, persuading, and communicating. You can learn 85% of what you need to learn to be successful in business from running a successful network marketing business.

Investing—Investing is the least time-consuming way to buy income-generating assets. You provide the finances and someone else does the work. It can be a way for you to participate in a business without being responsible for one.

You can be a millionaire. Let's assume that you could save 10% of your income and it would earn 10% a year between the ages of 25 and 55. That's one million dollars! Too bad none of us can stick to a budget. Here's the good news. If you follow your heart's desires and stick to your passion, you'll save more than 10% and God will show you returns much higher than 10%. Your cup really will overflow! I believe that is the message of II Corinthians 8–9.

The most common failure point—When Christians first get started on their passion, they usually get so excited and so ignited by the revelation of it all that they forget to get a little help. They use faith as an excuse to swim with the sharks, and they have a bad experience. Although you and your passion are as unique as a snowflake, you still can find someone who has covered some of the same ground before you who will save you years of mistakes. "Fathering" and networking are key ingredients in being Kingly. 100% of the people who are already wealthy know one thing that the rest of us may not—they can point to someone who helped them. Someone gave them an idea, did part of the work, or provided some of the financing. No one does it alone. Networking is a key ingredient to building wealth and converting money into ministry.

Haves and have nots—We determine our own level of prosperity. We decide this by our actions and attitudes toward money. If you decide to make a profit, you will find that multiplying the increase will come very easily. Think of it as being faithful with the resources God has entrusted to you to manage. Conversely, if you are too "spiritual" to manage money, you will grow poorer and poorer.

> *Take the talent from him and give it to the one who has the ten talents. For everyone who has will be given more, and he will have an abundance. Whoever does not have, even what he has will be taken from him.*
> (Matthew 25:28–30)

People who know how to multiply their talents usually have the following characteristics.

1. Manage (don't worship) your income-generating assets. They are your modern equivalent to talents that the Lord is inviting you to multiply.

2. Set your goals out for several years and then several decades, through the end of your life. Decide now what your inheritance goals are to pass along to your children after you're gone.

3. Avoid excessive spending on items that don't generate income (cars, houses, boats, etc.).

4. Be courageous and wise regarding your finances. Invest in your passion. Activate your heart and your creativity. Get excited! Enjoy your work.

5. Be persistent. Learn the lessons from your failures and plan your resurrections.

6. Bless the nations; be generous and leverage your assets to help others.

Giving—Why learn to prosper? It's a biblical way for Kings to multiply ministry. Giving really is more blessed and more fun than receiving. However, until you learn to receive and prosper, you won't have anything to give; more on that in the next section.

Resources–Here are a few resources you might enjoy. The first two web sites have many business tools and startup helps.

SCORE (Senior Core of Retired Executives) <u>www.score.org/</u> These are folks who are often Christians and have offices in most cities in the US. 375–3582

SBDC (Small Business Development Center) <u>www.wsbdc.org/</u> Many states have offices that provide help to small businesses just to develop the local economy. 547–0511

The Automatic Millionaire by David Bach is a secular book on saving money. I recommend "spending" on income-generating assets over saving, but this is still interesting reading. He recommends using your company matching savings to put money into your IRA to avoid taxes and save more than 10%.

KEY IV
I HAVE A PLAN FOR PRODUCTS—
ADDING VALUE TO THE LIVES OF OTHERS (MINISTRY)
EXERCISES AND QUESTIONS

It's very difficult to see yourself like God sees you. We're so close to ourselves, we don't always appreciate the awesome thing God is doing in our lives. Your life experiences, strategic people you know, and your blueprint DNA is a best-seller! The challenge is believing that you and God are writing this incredible script. When we live this way, our destiny is released!!!

1. Are you willing to allow others to help you? What kind of help do you need to make your dream come true? Who are the people that can add what you lack?

2. Can you see a personal Biblical connection between wealth and wisdom, "or" between wealth and spiritual maturity?

3. What do you know or do that has value for others?

4. How could you package this to effectively accelerate others in knowing what you know, and do what you're doing?

5. What do you do best? How can this skill fulfill a product for others?

KEY V
I'M MOVING FROM PROFITS TO PROSPERITY

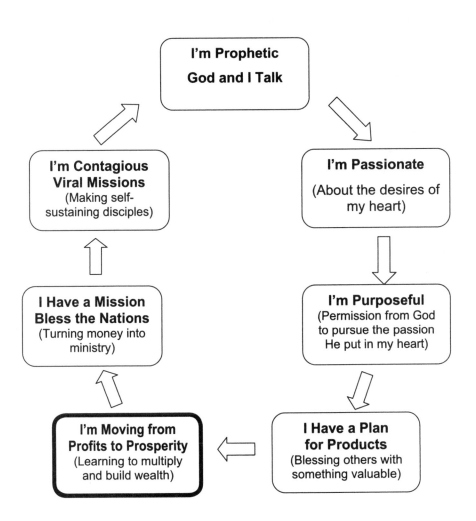

Wealth is a resource necessary to bless the nations. Money *won't be* magically transferred from the wicked into your pockets but it can be created with faith and a strategy. When used wisely, wealth is a tool that can magnify our ministry. We all share a responsibility and an anointing to multiply our talents and money.

Is wealth God's will? God actually gives us the ability to produce wealth. It's a gift and we can cultivate an anointing for it.

Wealth is a tool. Our goal isn't personal wealth; it's producing wealth that can be converted into ministry. We're not taking any of it with us, but we can produce wealth in this life and convert it into something that God really values—treasure in heaven.

A wealth mentality–Wealthy people do one thing others do not. They spend differently. They "shop" for income-generating assets instead of toys.

Breaking poverty–We're just as broke, whether we spend our money or give it to charity. Poverty is broken when you learn to "sow" your money and reap a return. Sustained giving comes from a position of abundance, from a cup that is overflowing.

Learn to multiply. God created us to "be fruitful and multiply." Learning to multiply money by sowing it led Isaac to a hundredfold increase. You can do it, too.

Put money to work. -Instead of working for money, God is teaching Kings to let money work for them.

CHAPTER 29
IS WEALTH GOD'S WILL?

With all the urgency and anointing of God's Spirit, the answer is an emphatic "YES!" The eyes of the Lord are searching throughout the earth for those who can handle wealth—those who can exercise their faith to receive it, and those with the wisdom to use it to build the Kingdom. The God of Abraham, Isaac, and Jacob is looking for Kings who are not ashamed to be blessed by God and promoted to new levels of influence and generosity.

> *But remember the* LORD *your God, for it is he who gives you the ability to produce wealth, and so confirms his covenant, which he swore to your forefathers, as it is today.* (Deuteronomy 8:17–18)

"Poor and humble" has been the goal of spirituality as defined by pastors and missionaries in the past (including me). Over the last few decades, the Church has transitioned through three major theological shifts. To be effective in ministry, you need three things: (1) salvation—including baptism, the Holy Spirit, etc.; (2) you need to be healthy; and (3) you need enough financial resources to carry out your ministry to bless others—more than enough. Let's consider each briefly.

1. **God's will is to see everyone saved.** Because not everyone responds to the Lord, we used to say it wasn't God's will for some. We don't hear that anymore! Even hearing that the Holy Spirit (tongues) isn't for everyone has diminished in evangelical debate.

> *For I take no pleasure in the death of anyone, declares the Sovereign* LORD. *Repent and live!*
> (Ezekiel 18:32)

This is good, and pleases God our Savior, who wants all men to be saved and to come to a knowledge of the truth. (I Timothy 2: 3–4)

The Lord is not slow in keeping his promise, as some understand slowness. He is patient with you, not wanting anyone to perish, but everyone to come to repentance. (II Peter 3:9)

2. Its God's will to see everyone healthy, and if they are sick, then He wants them healed. This is still a work in progress. You still hear people occasionally say that God is working through sickness. God's people have made lots of progress in healing over the last decade, because we're coming closer to understanding that God does want to heal us. Why isn't everyone healed? Same reason not everyone is saved—it's not God's fault nor design.

. . . by his wounds we are healed. (Isaiah 53:5)

He himself bore our sins in his body on the tree, so that we might die to sins and live for righteousness; by his wounds you have been healed. (I Peter 2:24)

3. God's will is to prosper His people. We're not even close on this one. Most of the body of Christ assume that wealth is a bigger curse than poverty. The level of deception on this front is amazing. So . . . we want to focus on this topic. Kings have to be comfortable with the biblical basis for receiving abundance from the hand of the Lord.

I am come that they might have life, and that they might have it more abundantly. (John 10:10 KJV)

*And God is able to make **all** grace abound to you, so that in **all things** at all times, having **all** that you*

*need, you will **abound** in every good work. As it is written: "He has scattered abroad his gifts to the poor; his righteousness endures forever." Now he who supplies seed to the sower and bread for food will also supply and increase your store of seed and will enlarge the harvest of your righteousness. You will be **made rich in every way** so that you can be **generous on every occasion**, and through us your generosity will result in thanksgiving to God.*
(II Corinthians 9: 8–11) [Emp. added]

Here God's will is articulated clearly. His grace **abounds** to you so that at **all** times you'll have **all** you need to **abound** to **every** good work. To water down that verse so that it doesn't include finances ignores the Old Testament pattern. Abraham, Isaac, Jacob, Joseph, David, Solomon, etc., were God's men and they were very prosperous.

And the LORD hath blessed my master [Abraham] greatly; and he is become great: and he hath given him flocks, and herds, and silver, and gold, and menservants, and maidservants, and camels, and asses.
(Genesis 24:35 KJV)

Isaac planted crops in that land and the same year reaped a hundredfold, because the LORD blessed him. The man became rich, and his wealth continued to grow until he became very wealthy. He had so many flocks and herds and servants that the Philistines envied him.
(Genesis 26:12–14)

Here's the will of God for you. He wants to prosper you beyond your needs to a place of abundance, so that you'll be in a position to fully understand His nature (God is abundant and generous), and so that you will be in a position to bless others. How? Checks are not going to start appearing mysteriously in the mail. You'll have to use faith, take risks, find an anointing for creativity, and you'll have to "work" diligently; making investments, starting a business, buying real estate. It's not magic but you'll be amazed at how God will multiply your efforts—100 fold.

Why prosperity? Jesus' atoning work on the cross includes salvation and healing. I want to suggest that it includes financial abundance as well. Most people understand that generosity is "good." What most of us miss is that God's heart is to bless us, as well. The main plank of the poverty mindset is that we are unworthy of God's abundance. What if all your needs were so exceedingly, abundantly met that instead of tithing 10%, you lived on 10% and used 90% to build the Kingdom?

> *For you know the grace of our Lord Jesus Christ, that though he was rich, yet for your sakes he became poor, so that you through his poverty might become rich.*
> (II Corinthians 8:9)

> *The Scripture foresaw that God would justify the Gentiles by faith, and announced the gospel in advance to Abraham: "**All nations will be blessed through you.**" So those who have faith are blessed along with Abraham, the man of faith.*
> (Galatians 3: 8–9 Refers to Genesis 12: 2–3, Abraham's covenant blessing.) [Emp. added]

> *Christ redeemed us from the curse of the law by becoming a curse for us, for it is written: "Cursed is everyone who is hung on a tree." **He redeemed us in order that the blessing given to Abraham might come to the Gentiles** through Christ Jesus, so that by faith we might receive the promise of the Spirit.*
> (Galatians 3:13–14) [Emp. added]

Here's the great commission. "All nations will be blessed through you." Something has changed in the Spirit. Our tradition is that people were called to the ministry or missions and then set about itinerating to raise the financial support to carry out their calling. God now is calling Kings to embrace abundant prosperity to "go" to the marketplace and "do" greater works. How we reach our cities and conduct missions in other nations will be very different and very exciting over the next ten years. God isn't calling just pastors, and prophets and missionaries—He's calling you! Kings who understand abundance will take expanding the Kingdom from theory to practice.

Here's a "teaser." What happens if I understand my gifts and calling for ministry but haven't found any financial release? Answer: I spend time and energy trying to influence others to support "my" vision with "their" finances. The inadvertent message is that others don't have a vision from God or at least don't have one as important as mine.

There is a reason for wealth. It does express God's generosity and His love for us. Money is also a "tool" that can be converted to ministry (treasure in heaven), as we will discuss in the next chapter.

CHAPTER 30
WEALTH IS A TOOL

We are targeting a group of people (namely you) with Kingly ministries. It really is God's purpose to channel great blessing through you. I will leave you to sort out how much is for you. I believe God lets us choose our course in a way that aligns with our gift-mix. Here are a couple of clear alternatives. You certainly won't be rejected for having less wealth than Bill Gates (however, Solomon makes Bill appear to be a pauper). I just want to swing back the curtain and ask if you can see abundance and generosity inside the will of God.

> *You will always have the poor among you, but you will not always have me.*
> (John 12:8)

> *For you know the grace of our Lord Jesus Christ, that though he was rich, yet for your sakes he became poor, so that you through his poverty might become rich.*
> (II Corinthians 8:9)

Fear #1–One of the biggest fears among Christians regarding wealth is a belief that it is forbidden, and it will lead to pride and a spectacular downfall. The following two verses could be used to make such a point. However, if you read them carefully, and in context, the real warning isn't against wealth; it's a warning against "the love of money" instead of the purposes for which it can be used.

> *By your wisdom and understanding you have gained wealth for yourself and amassed gold and silver in your treasuries. By your great skill in trading you have increased your wealth, and because of your wealth*

your heart has grown proud.

(Ezekiel 28: 4–5)

Be careful that you do not forget the LORD your God, failing to observe his commands, his laws and his decrees that I am giving you this day. Otherwise, when you eat and are satisfied, when you build fine houses and settle down, and when your herds and flocks grow large and your silver and gold increase and all you have is multiplied, then your heart will become proud and you will forget the LORD your God, who brought you out of Egypt, out of the land of slavery.

(Deuteronomy 8:11–14)

Greed and covetousness are real issues, but they are not the exclusive domain of the rich. In fact, the poor are more likely to succumb to envy and selfishness than the wealthy. Note that Solomon expresses his real heart's desire; to do a good job as a leader. I don't think that it takes a spiritual giant to realize that your calling or purpose should take priority over wealth, riches, honor, and long life. But please note that God doesn't withhold these things. In fact, they are His will (Genesis 12: 2–3). He just doesn't want us to worship them. Surely, that's not "too much to ask" nor "too hard to do."

God said to Solomon, "Since this is your heart's desire and you have not asked for wealth, riches or honor, nor for the death of your enemies, and since you have not asked for a long life but for wisdom and knowledge to govern my people over whom I have made you king, therefore wisdom and knowledge will be given you. And I will also give you wealth, riches and honor, such as no king who was before you ever had and none after you will have."   *(II Chronicles 1:11–12)*

Say it with me: "Producing wealth is God's will for me." Then read Deuteronomy 8:18 and realize it's part of His covenant promise. It's also the context for the warning in Deuteronomy 8:14, above.

Then, as you read the Bible, notice the multitude of verses and examples of people who used great wealth inside the will of God.

> *But remember the LORD your God, for it is he who gives you the ability to produce wealth, and so confirms his covenant, which he swore to your forefathers, as it is today.*
>
> (Deuteronomy 8:17–18)

The caveat on wealth and riches is summarized up in Matthew 6:33. Put His Kingdom first, and blessing, including the ability to produce wealth, will follow you where ever you go. The context of this verse is not just basic needs. Reading what precedes it, we are shown that even without a lot of toil, we are cared for better than Solomon. That's certainly beyond basic needs, in case you haven't read about Solomon lately. Remember all the wisdom . . . wealth . . . and what about those wives?

> *But seek first his kingdom and his righteousness, and all these things will be given to you as well. Therefore do not worry about tomorrow, for tomorrow will worry about itself. Each day has enough trouble of its own.*
>
> (Matthew 6:33–34)

The only thing that can stop wealth and blessing from flowing toward Kings is a belief that it's not God's will. Here's the reality, "Kings can't fill all the will of God without an abundance of money." Their generosity is part of their ministry.

Wealth is not forbidden; it is part of the will of God for you in your Kingly ministry. Now that we have that straight, you may be willing to permit God to add wealth to your walk. I want to take you a step farther regarding how God will give you financial increase.

> *Remember this: Whoever sows sparingly will also reap sparingly, and whoever sows generously will also reap generously. Each man should give what he has decided in his heart to give, not reluctantly or under*

*compulsion, for God loves a cheerful giver. And God
is able to make all grace abound to you, so that in all
things at all times, having all that you need, you will
abound in every good work.*

(II Corinthians 9:6–8)

The cheerful, brainless giver—We've all been taught that giving cheerfully is sowing seed and that whoever gives more will reap generously. We use this verse when we receive the offering in church. I believe it's time to teach the saints how to keep their pockets overflowing and give out of their abundance. Right now there is a severe tendency among the churched to feel guilty for having money or making money.

What is seed? How long does a farm last if all the seed is given away? One year! If you want to reap a harvest, you have to plant your seed. I want to suggest that the phrase "whoever sows generously will also reap generously" is pointing to the wisdom behind investments in things such as business or real estate. If as a King, you give away money that represents your seed, you can rest assured that you never will have any. Priests can—and probably should—give away their money, because God intends for them to live on the tithe. Kings who believe that offerings are going to be the answer to funding their ministries are a half bubble off into foolishness—it doesn't happen. Understanding cash flow, business opportunities, passive income, and wise investments is God's plan for sowing your seed. The ability to produce wealth and wisdom are connected in Scripture.

God supplies seed to plant. Notice in verse 10 that God supplies seed to the sower in such a way that increases the "store" of seed, and then the harvest of righteousness is enlarged. Why? The saint has something in his pocket to give. Listen to verse 11 and adopt it as your own goal, "I will be made rich in every way so that I can be generous on every occasion."

*Now he who supplies seed to the sower and bread for
food will also supply and increase your store of seed
and will enlarge the harvest of your righteousness.*

You will be made rich in every way so that you can be generous on every occasion, and through us your generosity will result in thanksgiving to God.
(II Corinthians 9:10–11) [Emp. added]

Kings and money—Here's the simple reality. Kings have to be comfortable with making and giving money. That's how the ministry of Kings works. They have to be wise enough not to give away their seed to sow. They must invest (sow or plant) it wisely. I believe there is an anointing available for Kings to receive great abundance. God is positioning them to do great things, and my prayer is that they don't put their seed in the offering plate. Tithe, yes; offerings, yes; seed, no. We can't view these truths as prescriptive principles which we blindly follow. However, we have to be open to the fact that God wants us to commune with Him at the level of our hearts' desires (as Solomon). He also wants Kings to want to make money and be open to the leading of the Holy Spirit as to how to accomplish it.

Treasure in heaven—Instead of merely tithing 10%, my personal goal is to live on 10% and have an overflow sized to give 90%. My goal isn't personal wealth; it's producing wealth that can be converted into ministry. We're not taking any of it with us, but we can produce wealth in this life and convert it into something that God really values—treasure in heaven.

> *Do not store up for yourselves treasures on earth, where moth and rust destroy, and where thieves break in and steal. But store up for yourselves treasures in heaven, where moth and rust do not destroy, and where thieves do not break in and steal. For where your treasure is, there your heart will be also.*
> (Matthew 6:19–21)

Here's your Kingly assignment. Produce wealth, multiply it one hundred fold, convert it to ministry along the way, and get the job done before you're called home . . . bless all nations.

To receive wealth so that we can operate out of a cup that runs over, we need a new mindset about money. In the next chapter we want to touch some very practical ways to view wealth.

CHAPTER 31
MOVING TO A WEALTH MENTALITY

"**Wealth**" as a term often is reserved for a small class of people who live lavish and excessive lifestyles. There was a TV show called *Lifestyles of the Rich and Famous* that catered to the curious envy many of us have for rich people. I'd like to take the wall down and show how you can touch wealth as well. After all, it's God's idea—especially for Kings.

> *But remember the LORD your God, for it is he who gives you the ability to produce wealth, and so confirms his covenant, which he swore to your forefathers, as it is today.* (Deuteronomy 8:18)

> *The blessing of the LORD brings wealth, and he adds no trouble to it.* (Proverbs 10:22)

It has helped me to see my "poverty mentality" by contrasting it with those who are accustomed to wealth. Each class views money differently.

> **Lower class**—These folks get a paycheck at the end of their bi-weekly work period and use it to buy stuff. The favorite purchases are a new TV, a better used car, or things for the house. Whenever they have money, they spend it on "stuff."

> **Middle class**—This income group is often college educated and can have relatively high-paying jobs. Whatever the income level is, spending is adjusted upward. The distinction from the lower class is credit.

These folks can borrow money and make payments on "bigger stuff," such as boats, vacations, new cars, new homes, and second homes. Their toys are adjusted up until their payments match their income.

Wealthy—By outward appearances, these folks actually don't look noticeably different from middle or lower class people. However, instead of having a priority on "stuff," they buy income generating assets. In other words, they buy things that make more money. Their purchase might be a business, an investment, or real estate. Their focus is on being entrepreneurial instead of working for another person's company.

Generosity—This comparison is simplistic but it does make a real world distinction between wealth and riches. All three classes spend money (riches), but only the wealthy have assets that generate income. Even less affluent families spend around $100,000 a year. That approaches $10M in riches spent over a lifetime. Please note one more distinction. Lower and middle class people are generally always "cash poor." They don't have the flexibility to be generous. Christians in each of those classes can be taught to tithe, in the sense that paying the Lord is just one more bill; only it's at the top of the list. But, they simply don't have the resources available to be truly generous. The Holy Spirit can drop hints all day long about financing a need, and it is simply a leading to which they (usually "we") can't respond. By contrast, wealthy people can always leverage cash and credit to buy another income-generating asset or respond to a financial need. They have the ability to be givers instead of just tithers.

The result—People with a wealth mentality can take talents given to them by the Lord, double them, and give them back. What if you give a talent to someone with a lower or middle class mentality? It either will get spent or it will get buried until needed because they are not theologically able to use assets to generate more assets. They punch the clock at work and spend their money.

Your assignment—Regardless of your financial status, scrape up enough cash to buy your first income-generating asset. I could list examples, but it would be better if you made it a matter of prayer and allowed the Holy Spirit to lead you. Next time you want to really help a ministry, instead of giving them cash, give them the ongoing proceeds from one of your income-generating assets. God has promised to give you the power to produce wealth without adding a lot of trouble to it. It's part of your "new land" waiting for your faith to rise to a level where you can posses it.

Ramifications—Now, for a moment imagine that you have wealth—assets that generate income. Most companies realize their greatest asset is their employees. Imagine that you have employees whom you disciple to double their talents. Get it? Employees are income-generating assets! Not in the robotic sense, of course. What if Kings disciple their employees to accumulate wealth? Your ability to expand the Kingdom would be multiplied greatly. We are not changing merely your fruitfulness, we're changing the way you disciple others, so that your spiritual sons and daughters are generous and gifted, both spiritually and financially.

Inheritance—There is one last ingredient of the wealth mentality. If you have income-generating assets in your estate, they can be passed on to your children. Imagine your labor expanding the Kingdom continuing on through your children and grandchildren long after you've gone home to be with the Lord!

> *A good man leaves an inheritance for his children's children, but a sinner's wealth is stored up for the righteous.* (Proverbs 13:22)

It's very simple. Wealth spends riches on wealth-producing assets, while the rest of us buy cars. Let's talk about breaking a poverty mentality in the next chapter.

CHAPTER 32
HOW TO BREAK POVERTY

Giving and receiving—As a pastor, I was blessed to have a church full of people who tithed. We bought and paid for a building that seated 200 people in five years, supported missions, and paid staff counselors. I prided myself in encouraging people to be generous. There is nothing wrong with that, except I never taught people how to make money; a clear promise in Scripture—especially for Kings. We also must think of it as a covenant promise; part of what Jesus provided via the cross.

> *But thou shalt remember the LORD thy God: for it is he that giveth thee power to get wealth, that he may establish his covenant which he sware unto thy fathers, as it is this day.*
>
> (Deuteronomy 8:18 KJV)

> *Isaac planted crops in that land and **the same year reaped a hundredfold, because the LORD blessed him**. The man became rich, and his wealth continued to grow until he became very wealthy. He had so many flocks and herds and servants that the Philistines envied him.*
>
> (Genesis 26:12–14) [Emp. added]

> *For you know the grace of our Lord Jesus Christ, that though he was rich, yet for your sakes he became poor, so that you through his poverty **might become rich**.*
>
> (II Corinthians 8: 8–9) [Emp. added]

Poverty causes money to flee. During my pastoral days, when it was time to take the offering my favorite verse was "give and it shall be given to you." (Luke 6:38) The implication is that if you want God to bless you financially, you should put your money in the offering. Here's what I've learned since. Poverty is a spirit or mentality that causes money to leave people. Many Christians are uncomfortable allowing any money to accumulate in their possession. They believe if money does come their way, that it's spiritual to give it away, believing that God will give it back. "You can't out-give God," you know (**not** in the Bible). What was absent in my pastoral instruction was how to multiply finances. I taught people to give, I taught people to save, budget, and how to be good stewards. But, I had no message that taught them how to multiply finances. In fact, I unknowingly kept them in poverty.

An anointing to multiply—I believe in anointing. It's been a blessing to see the anointing for healing increase on God's people over the years. We used to pray for people; nothing happened and we weren't surprised. Now it seems the Lord touches every one who receives prayer in some way. The same is true for prophecy. Several decades ago it was just for prophets. Now most of God's people can receive words and share them with great effect. I see the same thing happening with finances. God is opening a door to multiply finances. There is an anointing to do it and the truth that sets people free is that it's OK to multiply finances. In fact, it's part of the ministry package necessary to reach the world. You see, money can be converted to ministry! Pretty amazing isn't it?

> *Now he who supplies seed to the sower and bread for food will also supply and **increase your store of seed** and will enlarge the harvest of your righteousness. **You will be made rich in every way so that you can be generous on every occasion,** and through us your generosity will result in thanksgiving to God.*
> (II Corinthians 9:10–11) [Emp. added]

And here's how—What do businessmen know that most of God's people miss? Money is multiplied by investing it. Notice the promise above to increase your store of seed. Many Christians give away their seed and have nothing to plant, so there is nothing to multiply. Every believer needs financial seed to sow and a plan to multiply finances.

What happens when you give all your money away, expecting God to multiply it back miraculously? Nothing, except you're broke. Remember, that's the definition of a poverty mentality. All the money goes away. TV preachers are an exception to this. No matter how much they give, the people watching send more. My suggestion is that you invest your money, at least until you get your own TV show.

Jacob and God had a covenant for giving. Jacob didn't just give God a tenth of everything he had. He vowed he would give a tenth of **the increase** that God gave him. For every $100,000 Jacob gave, he kept $900,000. That strikes me as a good deal for everybody. In the new covenant we're not limited to 10%. We can be prosperous enough to live well on 10% and give 90%.

> *Then Jacob made a vow, saying, "If God will be with me and will watch over me on this journey I am taking and will give me food to eat and clothes to wear so that I return safely to my father's house, then the LORD will be my God and this stone that I have set up as a pillar will be God's house, and of all that you give me I will give you a tenth."*
>
> (Genesis 28:20–22)

The mindset (poverty vs. abundance)—People have several views on all the promises of abundance and prosperity in the Bible. Some view them as belonging to Israel. Others view them as God's favor on the Church. God has and will favor both Israel and the Church through Christ. However, I think all those promises belong to individuals through whom God will bring His favor. Great blessing is available now, but God has committed Himself to move through people such as you. He wants to bless you so you in turn can be a blessing.

> *I will make you into a great nation and I will bless*
> *you; I will make your name great, and you will be a*
> *blessing. I will bless those who bless you, and whoever*
> *curses you I will curse; and all peoples on earth will be*
> *blessed through you.*
>
> (Genesis 12: 2–3)

This is a prophetic hour. God is inviting us to move from a poverty mindset into an abundant mindset so that we can multiply—finances, ministries, blessings, and salvations. You're being invited to choose the favor of God; choose to receive; choose to multiply.

Poverty—See how little can I spend; how much can I save? (I'm afraid I'll lose it.)

> *But the man who had received the one talent went off,*
> *dug a hole in the ground and hid his master's money.*
> (Matthew 25:18)

Abundance—See how can I multiply what I already have? (I want the blessing so I can be a blessing.)

> *The man who had received the five talents went at once*
> *and put his money to work and gained five more.*
> (Matthew 25:16)

You can multiply your seed if: (1) you realize God is favoring you to do so; (2) you have a good seed-planting work ethic; and (3) you realize God is blessing you so that you can release others from a poverty mentality . . . not just giving money, but discipling multiplication. Now let's learn how to move from addition to multiplication.

CHAPTER 33
LEARNING TO MULTIPLY

So God created man in his own image, in the image of God created he him; male and female created he them. And God blessed them, and God said unto them, **Be fruitful, and multiply,** *and replenish the earth, and subdue it: and have dominion . . .*
(Genesis 1:27–28 KJV) [Emp. added]

There are four basic ingredients of multiplication: God's favor, working smarter, sowing, and giving.

1. You can have God's favor. Americans love to believe that God doesn't play favorites—all men are created equal. I do think that we all have the same opportunity to please the Father, but that's where equality ends. God clearly delights in certain attributes and clearly favors the ones who display those attributes. Listen to Joseph's testimony.

The LORD was with him; he showed him kindness and granted him favor in the eyes of the prison warden. So the warden put Joseph in charge of all those held in the prison, and he was made responsible for all that was done there. **The warden paid no attention to anything under Joseph's care,** *because the LORD was with Joseph and gave him success in whatever he did.*
(Genesis 39:21–23) [Emp. added]

Why did God favor Joseph? It was because the warden didn't have to worry about anything under Joseph's care. He was diligent, faithful, hard working, and believing God through decades of setbacks and delays. Just as Joseph, you probably already have received your share of setbacks and delays. The attribute that attracts the favor of God is your tenacity to remain a good steward of the opportunities you do have. Compare Joseph with the parable of the sower.

> *. . . But the one who received the seed that fell on good soil is the man who hears the word and understands it.* **He produces a crop,** *yielding a hundred, sixty or thirty times what was sown.*
>
> (Matthew 13:23) [Emp. added]

God favors those who "produce a crop." We see the same bias in the Parable of the Talents. Notice the phrase, "put his money to work." He worked smarter and multiplied.

> *The man who had received the five talents went at once and* **put his money to work** *and gained five more.*
>
> (Matthew 25:16) [Emp. added]

God's favor was not on the servant who returned the one talent he was given. In fact, the parable only can be interpreted to mean that God gets frustrated with slothful servants. The terminology is "wicked, lazy, and worthless servant." (Matthew 25:26, 30) Want God's favor? Work harder and smarter.

2. Working smarter—Most of us have read II Corinthians 9:6.

> *Remember this: Whoever sows sparingly will also reap sparingly, and whoever sows generously will also reap generously.*
>
> (II Corinthians 9:6)

What we "hear" from the verse goes something similar to this, "Whoever **gives** sparingly will also reap sparingly." I think Paul was careful in his language and meant what he said. Sowing is not giving, it's planting with an expectation of a crop; it's investing or purchasing an income-producing asset to multiply your seed; putting your money to work. Paul was positioning people to have wealth over the course of at least a year (II Corinthians 8:10, 9:2) so that they could give. We've misconstrued the verse to skip sowing our seed so that it can multiply. Let's be clear about this.

Right now you can empty your checking account for your favorite ministry and expect blessing from God. Would you receive it? Probably not, because you skipped an important, practical part of the process—sowing your seed. Here are a couple of examples.

> *Isaac planted crops in that land and **the same year reaped a hundredfold**, because the LORD blessed him. The man became rich, and his wealth continued to grow until he became very wealthy. He had so many flocks and herds and servants that the Philistines envied him.*
> (Genesis 26:12–14) [Emp. added]

What if you planted your seed (invested your money) and received a hundredfold return in one year? At that point you would be positioned to give. Most Christians struggle with receiving wealth and give out of guilt instead of generosity. The result is that bills don't get paid and giving remains small and sacrificial—and giving is no fun! You cannot give cheerfully when your gift is competing with a creditor for the same money.

3. Sowing Your Talents (Matthew 25:14) and Minas (Luke 19:12). The faithful steward "at once put his money to work." He's sowing with the expectation of a harvest. He's letting his money do the work of multiplication. The reward for multipling one talent into five is "put in charge of many things." In Luke our servants are put in charge of cities. Sounds like Kings taking their position in city transformation doesn't it?

The other promise is, "Come and share your master's happiness." Multiplication is fun. It blessed God's heart and it results in the joy of the Lord. Kings are blessed and happy.

So why do we have a servant who simply keeps his talent and gets an incredible label, "wicked and lazy servant?" Listen to his concept of master (often our concept of God). The master is accused of harvesting where he has not sown.

> *Then the man who had received the one talent came.
> "Master," he said, "I knew that you are a hard man,
> **harvesting where you have not sown and gathering
> where you have not scattered seed.** So I was afraid
> and went out and hid your talent in the ground. See,
> here is what belongs to you."*
> (Matthew 25:24–25 see also Luke 19:20–21)
> [Emp. added]

What is a little surprising is that this concept of the master is not refuted.

> *His master replied, "You wicked, lazy servant! So
> you knew that **I harvest where I have not sown and
> gather where I have not scattered seed?** Well then,
> you should have put my money on deposit with the
> bankers, so that when I returned I would have re-
> ceived it back with interest."*
> (Matthew 25:26–27, Luke 19:22)

Here's the surprising reality. God is not a hard man unless you bury your talent. He does reap where He hasn't sown. Want to know why? We are the ones that are supposed to sow the seed and God is the one that does the multiplication . . . no sowing; no multiplication; no harvest. Listen to Paul's version of sowing and reaping.

> *I planted the seed, Apollos watered it, but God made
> it grow.* (I Corinthians 3:6)

We sow; God gives the increase. We're the fuse, God's the bomb. We're the match, God's the forest fire. We're the witness, God's the One who saves people. We sow something relatively small and God does something really big with our initiative. If you want to experience mul- tiplication, you have to sow something that God can multiply. Be wary of being too spiritual. The context of Matthew 25 is "property" (Mat- thew 25:14). We call it real estate. If we confuse "giving" and "sowing" we might accidentally land in the "wicked, lazy servant" category.

It's Time—It takes courage, wisdom, and a mentor to learn to multiply by "sowing" into real estate, investing or starting a business. Most Christians have been programmed by their theology to "pass" on these "carnal" activities. It's time to say, "Yes Lord" and multiply some talents so we can have a harvest.

4. Giving—God does favor generosity. It's part of who He is and it reflects His "cattle on a thousand hills" abundance. We've been taught that "spiritual people" give out of their poverty and have faith for miraculous provisions. I think that is mostly a combination of religious pride and a poverty mentality. Real spiritual giving comes from people who have learned to tap an anointing for abundance . . . "rich in every way so you too can be generous on every occasion." They prepared in advance by planting, harvesting, and increasing their seed.

> *Now he who supplies seed to the sower and bread for food will also supply and increase your store of seed and will enlarge the harvest of your righteousness. You will be made rich in every way so that you can be generous on every occasion, and through us your generosity will result in thanksgiving to God.*
> (II Corinthians 9:10–11) [Emp. added]

In summary:

- God favors those who are faithful (Josephs).

- We can work a lot "smarter" by sowing our seed in income generating assets that multiply.

- The joy of giving is the frosting that goes with abundance. God wants you rich in every way so you can be generous on every occasion.

CHAPTER 34
PUTTING MONEY TO WORK

Instead of working for money (some call it a "wage slave"), we're learning to put money to work and let it work for us.

Step 1—Sow. Sow the seed by putting your money to work in an investment that will yield a harvest. Sow "bountifully."

> *The man who had received the five talents went at once and put his money to work and gained five more.*
> (Matthew 25:16)

> *But this I say, He which soweth sparingly shall reap also sparingly; and* ***he which soweth bountifully shall reap also bountifully.***
> (II Corinthians 9:6 KJV) [Emp. added]

Step 2—Multiply. Find the way God promises to "multiply your seed sown." The NIV says "increase your store of seed." Translation, "Christians making money" (the power to produce wealth, Deuteronomy 8:18).

> *Now he that ministereth seed to the sower both minister bread for your food, and* ***multiply your seed sown,*** *and increase the fruits of your righteousness). . . .*
> (II Corinthians 9:10 KJV) [Emp. added]

Step 3—Harvest. See the harvest from your planting. Isaac multiplied his investment 100 fold in the same year (that's 10,000% interest!).

> *Isaac planted crops in that land and the same year reaped a hundredfold, because the LORD blessed him.*

> *The man became rich, and his wealth continued to grow until he became very wealthy. He had so many flocks and herds and servants that the Philistines envied him.*
>
> (Genesis 26:12–14)

Step 4—Tithe and give offerings. Invest first and give out of your increase. One of the great deceptions of our time is that God wants you to give until you're broke. Giving does open the floodgates of heaven. Do be generous; but don't be foolish and give away your seed for sowing.

> *"Bring the whole tithe into the storehouse, that there may be food in my house. Test me in this," says the LORD Almighty, "and see if I will not throw open the floodgates of heaven and pour out so much blessing that you will not have room enough for it. I will prevent pests from devouring your crops, and the vines in your fields will not cast their fruit," says the LORD Almighty. "Then all the nations will call you blessed, for yours will be a delightful land," says the LORD Almighty."* (Malachi 3:10–12)

Times and seasons The Lord is anointing Kings to multiply. Multiplication is actually one of God's original blessings that begins in the Garden of Eden and is repeated often. We're in a season when the eyes of the Lord are searching throughout the earth to find Kings who are willing to sow with faith to multiply a return on their investments so they have the wealth it takes to really expand the Kingdom. As we discussed in a previous chapter, *Wealth is a Tool* . . . please do not give away your seed. Multiply it, give from a position of abundance, and sow seed again for a future harvest. An investment is a gift that keeps on giving because money has been put to work. Be fruitful and multiply!

> *And God blessed them, saying,* ***Be fruitful, and multiply****, and fill the waters in the seas, and let fowl multiply*

in the earth.
(Genesis 1:22 KJV) [Emp. added]

And God blessed them, and God said unto them, ***Be fruitful, and multiply.* . . .**
(Genesis 1:28 KJV) [Emp. added]

. . . ***be fruitful, and multiply*** *upon the earth.*
(Genesis 8:17 KJV) [Emp. added]

And God blessed Noah and his sons, and said unto them, ***Be fruitful, and multiply.* . . .**
(Genesis 9:1 KJV) [Emp. added]

And you, ***be ye fruitful, and multiply;*** *bring forth abundantly in the earth, and multiply therein.*
(Genesis 9:7 KJV) [Emp. added]

And when Abram was ninety years old and nine, the LORD *appeared to Abram, and said unto him, I am the Almighty God; walk before me, and be thou perfect. And I will make my covenant between me and thee, and* ***will multiply thee exceedingly.***
(Genesis 17: 1–2 KJV) [Emp. added]

For when God made promise to Abraham, because he could swear by no greater, he sware by himself, Saying, Surely blessing I will bless thee, ***and multiplying I will multiply thee.***
(Hebrews 6:13–14 KJV) [Emp. added]

But the one who received the seed that fell on good soil is the man who hears the word and understands it. ***He produces a crop, yielding a hundred, sixty or thirty times what was sown.***
(Matthew 13:23) [Emp. added]

Sow your seed. God has positioned Red Rock Energy and people such as Mike and Dan with opportunities to help you multiply.

Now the exciting part—imagine yourself with an abundance of resources and life. What would you do? After the shock wore off, you would find the greatest pleasure in doing whatever it is that God is doing in the earth. He's busy "blessing the nations."

KEY V
MOVING FROM PROFITS TO PROSPERITY
WHAT'S YOUR PROSPERITY QUOTIENT?
EXERCISES AND QUESTIONS

Let's not be overly spiritual. We can measure what we believe. God says our words, attitudes, and actions should say the same as His. For too long, we have all played the game of "saying the right thing," and then acting like we have amnesia after. No wonder we feel disjointed. Kings are beginning to align their hearts, their words, and their actions. It feels a lot healthier inside; new creativity and energy are the result of an integrated life.

1. If you believe God is calling you to prosper in the marketplace, aspire to surround yourself with business mentors who are further along than you. Why is this important?

2. Successful people in sports have coaches and personal trainers. What specific coaching and mentoring do you need?

3. Who could you take to lunch this week to download the wisdom and anointing you need? Identify 10 people you don't think you deserve to walk with. Call them up anyway and ask for help.

4. What kind of coaching tools and mentoring would you like to participate in?

5. If we put a "wealth measuring device" on your mouth and your heart, how wealthy are you? For "out of the abundance of the heart, the mouth speaks."

KEY VI
I HAVE A MISSION—
BLESS THE NATIONS

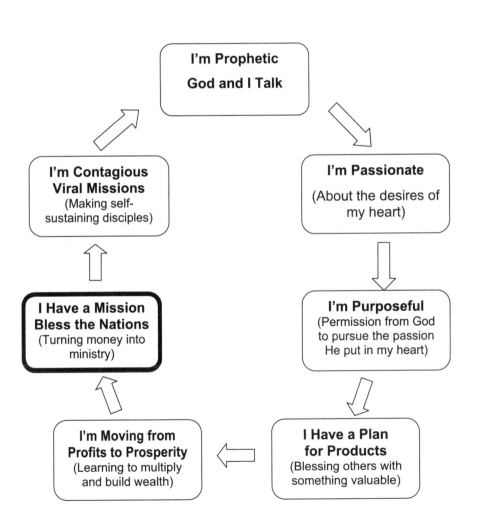

I'm Prophetic
God and I Talk

I'm Contagious
Viral Missions
(Making self-
sustaining disciples)

I'm **Passionate**
(About the desires of
my heart)

I Have a Mission
Bless the Nations
(Turning money into
ministry)

I'm **Purposeful**
(Permission from God
to pursue the passion
He put in my heart)

I'm **Moving from
Profits to Prosperity**
(Learning to multiply
and build wealth)

I Have a Plan
for Products
(Blessing others with
something valuable)

"Mission" happens when our passion, purpose, products, and prosperity align with God's plan for the Kingdom, and we begin exporting from a cup that is running over. God is using Kings to bless the nations, not only with the gospel and planting churches, but He's redeeming entire economies and raising families, communities, and nations to abundant life in every area.

In addition to using evangelists, their organizations, and church networks, God is launching a grassroots groundswell of Kings who are operating out of the desires of their hearts to expand the Kingdom. In this section we've highlighted a few examples, and we close with a suggestion on how you can launch the passion God has placed in your own heart.

Turning money into ministry—Money is a tool that is entirely necessary to do the will of God. To have money and ministry, you have to be willing to multiply the talents God has given you. Many try to go straight to ministry without money, and they end in offering cycles, asking others to fund their visions. For Kings, God is showing people how to multiply their finances and using their increase to expand ministries in the Kingdom.

Blessing the nations—The US historically has had a national call to missions that extends right into the future (we're not the only nation). It's part of why we're blessed. Intertwined with that national destiny is a marketplace ministry influence on building the Kingdom.

Write your own ticket. The most important ingredient that would help God's people become Kings is "initiative." We theologically underestimate the roles God wants us to play in implementing our hearts' desires and deciding what voluntary roles we could present to Jesus as gifts to help build the Kingdom. While millions of servants are asking the Lord, "What do you want me to do?" the Lord is looking for friends who will see and share His heart and lovingly *propose,* "What they would like to do for Jesus."

CHAPTER 35
CONVERTING MONEY INTO MINISTRY

I want to share what's happening with Mike Nelson. He's converting money into ministry, something Kings do well.

> *For you know the grace of our Lord Jesus Christ, that though he was rich, yet for your sakes he became poor, so that you through his poverty might become rich.*
> (II Corinthians 8:9)

> *And God is able to make all grace abound to you, so that in all things at all times, having all that you need, you will abound in every good work.*
> (II Corinthians 9:8)

> *You will be made rich in every way so that you can be generous on every occasion . . .*
> (II Corinthians 9:11)

Red rock energy—Mike and Dan Griffin have a modest oil well business in Texas and a vision to support ministry. 2005 was a tough year, even though oil prices were up, because well drilling rigs all were occupied by the large companies. Red Rock is organized with one wing of the company called Red Rock Ministries. Ten percent of the gross is used to support a number of different ministries, shown on their web site. They also have a gas well called Jireh #1 that was drilled in 2002 in which three shares of the well were given to three of their partner ministries. That well has been up and down, but declined in the last part of 2005, so they shot the well (opened it up to another level). The result . . . production went up 40 fold, from 830 MCF to over 30,000. It's even producing 100 barrels of oil a week. It was a prophetic message . . . the 40-fold increase points to the end of their season in the wilderness. They believe in creating significant income streams for ministry.

The personality—Mike and Dan have huge hearts for ministry. Although they both can preach and teach, they believe they are called primarily to give themselves to business, so eventually they can reach a point of supporting ministry with 90% of their income. These guys are having fun, and they routinely see one divine appointment after another. God is working with them!

A new drilling rig—Although they have a dozen wells in production and a base of 120 investors (mostly Christians), Red Rock growth depends on drilling new wells. In 2005, investors were calling asking about new opportunities, but no drilling rigs were available, and the waiting list to have one built was a year long. So they began seeking the Lord and ran into a series of divine appointments. Many contacts came through friends and business relationships where God brought them the answer through another person. Other people are seeing the hand of God behind their progress and jumping in on the divine appointments as though it were a revival.

1.   They made a decision to build their own drilling rig through contacts the Lord had given them who had prior experience.

2.   They were introduced to a young man (a welder) who recently was saved who is their shop foreman.

3.   They needed a place to build a rig, which could have entailed purchasing land and building a shop. The Lord led them to a local shop, and the owner is letting them use it free, in exchange for doing some of the work fabricating the rig.

4.   Mike also has been introduced to contacts in the industry who have experience in drilling, so he's staffing the operating crew. Many involved are Christians, and times of intercession have been a trademark of their miraculous progress.

5.   Enjoy the story so far? Everything came to a screeching halt at the shop and ended up in court. Mike's response—he rented another drilling rig to drill the well and hit a major gas reservoir. He

could have wilted, but he found a way around this problem.

6. The rig in construction will soon be drilling and returning 40% for investors who provided $4M in capital via a Limited Partnership. The completed rig has an appraised value of $6M, so the investors will start with $2M in equity.

7. The stage is set to build more rigs. Mike was given a prophetic word that they wouldn't just have one rig but three.

Can it happen for you? I don't see Red Rock as an isolated event. Kings are making breakthroughs all over the world. Here are four key ingredients.

1. Find the desire of your heart (and God's heart). Red Rock is making money and their prosperity is staged to multiply. But the foundation isn't just built on making money; it resides on a call Mike and Dan carry for supporting missions. They are building the Kingdom and having fun doing it even through the warfare.

> *But seek first his kingdom and his righteousness, and all these things will be given to you as well.*
> (Matthew 6:33–34 NIV)

> *When the disciples saw this, they were amazed. "How did the fig tree wither so quickly?" they asked. Jesus replied, "I tell you the truth, if you have faith and do not doubt, not only can you do what was done to the fig tree, but also you can say to this mountain, Go, throw yourself into the sea, and it will be done. If you believe, you will receive whatever you ask for in prayer."*
> (Matthew 21:20–22)

2. Don't be afraid of money. Money is a tool that is entirely necessary to do the will of God. To have money and ministry, you have to be willing to multiply the talents God has given to you. Many try to go straight to ministry without money, and they end in an offering cycle, asking others to fund their vision. For Kings, God is showing people how to multiply their finances and using their increase to expand ministry in the Kingdom. One of my personal desires is to help Christians network with opportunities such as Red Rock. forty percent returns are for everyone; so is ministry. Generosity is the goal, but it doesn't start until you've learned how to multiply your finances and have something to give.

3. Ask, and keep on asking. I used to define spirituality in terms of "spiritual" things—no longer. I really believe that maturity in Kings is measured partially by our entrepreneurial quotient; our ability to multiply finances. It's an anointing that God is unveiling right now. Please don't feel disqualified by your present poverty. It's a season to "ask," just as Mike did. God is answering! You, too, can be trusted with "much."

> *Whoever can be trusted with very little can also be* ***trusted with much,*** *and whoever is dishonest with very little will also be dishonest with much. So if you have not been trustworthy in handling worldly wealth, who will trust you with true riches? And if you have not been trustworthy with someone else's property, who will give you property of your own?*
>
> (Luke 16:10–12) [Emp. added]

4. Get started. Most people retire with several hundred thousand dollars in their pension, IRA's, etc. Then, they live right at the poverty level on a monthly stipend which represents well under 10% return on their hard-earned capital. Investments such as Red Rock represent a 10-fold increase over that "safely in poverty" mentality. Do the math.

CHAPTER 36
THIRD WORLD MISSIONS—
STARFISH STYLE

"The starfish doesn't have a head. Its central body isn't even in charge. In fact, the major organs are replicated throughout each and every arm. If you cut an arm off, most of these animals grow a new arm. Linckia, or long-armed starfish, can replicate itself from just a single piece of an arm. You can cut the Linckia into a bunch of pieces, and each one will regenerate a whole new starfish. They can achieve this magical regeneration because in reality, a starfish is neural network—basically a network of cells. The starfish functions as a decentralized network."

From *The Starfish and the Spider*
by Ori Brafman and Rod Beckstrom

Christians are a little like the starfish. Each member of the body of Christ carries the whole blueprint for God's plan because we each carry God Himself within us (the Holy Spirit). God is speaking to the hearts of individuals to step into their heart's desire and pursue the Kingdom. Some operate within the hierarchy of organizational oversight and others operate like the starfish—they just "do the stuff" under the leadership of the Holy Spirit and within the scope of their hearts desire. It's amazing what one little leg can do.

Duane Smith (real estate agent) and Howard Ferris (civil engineer) both have organized crusades and conferences that started with e-mail contacts. Here's what is absolutely amazing. They are normal people who have taken a Kingly initiative in third-world missions, to the tune of 60,000 salvations and training for several thousand pastors. They are inspiring examples of what you can do, as well.

Here's the God-side of the equation. The US historically has had a national call to missions that extends right into the future (we're not the only nation). It's part of why we're blessed. Intertwined with that national destiny is a marketplace ministry influence on building the Kingdom. God is using people from the business world to expand His Kingdom. These examples (crusades and church plants) will eventually extend to the release of Kings and prosperity (self-supporting missions) in those same nations. If you've never been to a third-world nation for ministry, it's amazing. Healings, salvations, teaching . . . it's rolling off a log. Anyone with a modest level of maturity can move in the miraculous, because God's heart is directed toward those needs.

Help us! Nearly all ministry web sites generate inquiries from pastors inviting outside help (ours, too). Not all of the inquiries are legitimate, and they have to be funded by those who go at costs that range from $10–$30,000. That's why these requests usually end in the trash. Few churches or ministries have the staff or the budget to respond. However, Duane and Howard have taken several trips. We want to highlight their experience in developing these relationships for a very simple reason. There are thousands of these kinds of requests that need attention, and I believe there are thousands of Kings out there who could do the job with a little encouragement.

I asked Duane and Howard to outline their approach to exploring recent trips to India and the Philippines. These are four suggestions.

1. Start small—Weeding through many e-mail requests and choosing people of similar heart with whom to build a relationship is challenging. Faith, patience, and a divine appointment are mandatory ingredients. I build relationships as a first priority. From a relationship, I look at ways to get involved and co-labor in their "field of ministry." Before any consideration of a crusade or ministry trip, the relationship is seasoned by time (usually a few months) and smaller joint participation projects that validate the genuineness of their dedication to building His Kingdom, not their own. Pictures of their churches and outreach programs assist in validating their situation. With Pastor Anil in India and Pastor Bonifar in the Philippines, we built financial accountability by sending money for Bible purchases and orphan/widow assistance. Receipts and pictures of Bibles, clothing, and food distribution were required to proceed to the next level of confidence. In both cases, their hearts for Kingdom work became very apparent.

2. Scope of the trip—Second, the scope of what could be done with the contact you have needs to be evaluated. This is harder to assess. Some questions that need good answers are: "Do you have other pastors who will assist you in holding a crusade?" "What is your follow-up plan?" "Do you have the resources and people to birth a new church or incorporate the new believers into your existing churches?"

3. Budget the cost—A line-item budget needs to be made and followed. We requested the pastors make a detailed budget, including equipment rentals, transportation, facilities, government permits, and team accommodations, to name a few. Pictures of the hotel are imperative. Their idea of reasonable accommodations and yours are probably different. The budget will vary greatly by the size and scope of the mission. The two-day crusade in the Philippines cost about $1,000. This was a lower budget crusade, with minimal advertising and one truck rental to haul people. The three-day pastors' conference cost about $5,000 (including meals and travel for the attendees). The outreach, including airline tickets for two, totaled about $11,000. Our India trip in April was almost twice that budget. A $20–$30K budget should be adequate to conduct a larger crusade (20,000–50,000 people), similar to the crusades that Howard conducted in Pakistan. Adding a pastors' conference will increase your influence but also greatly increase your cost (few indigenous pastors have the ability to provide for their own travel, accommodations, and meals).

Howard's estimate—In approximate terms, our first Pakistan trip in September, 2005 (three one-day crusades), cost $15,000 and reached 24,000 for Christ ($0.63/salvation). Our second trip in August 2006, cost $34,000 and reached about 30,000 ($1.18/salvation). During our second trip, one crusade meeting was cancelled due to rain; the expected attendance was 25,000. For very rough estimates, $1 per salvation is a good approximation for India or Pakistan right now. I understand that the cost per convert based on moneys given to the Church in the USA exceeds $100,000 per salvation. While I can't substantiate this, I know it is very high. In terms of Kingdom economics, the greater return is in the troubled, unreached nations of the world.

4. Resources—O'Dell Ministries has some excellent practical publications on preaching the gospel with signs, wonders, and miracles, which is mandatory for reaching the unevangelized populations of the world. Howard has been to one of their crusade training seminars. They also have an excellent booklet on the simple presentation of the gospel They have held hundreds of crusades and have reached over 13 million for Christ in India, Pakistan, and Honduras. Howard has also has used their resources with great success. Howard used the House Church planting model to follow his crusades in India.

How did they afford it? Duane and Howard have funded and organized these missions trips themselves. Portions of their recent trips have been supported by friends or church offerings (the recent Philippine trip was funded primarily by Duane's church, Desert Rock). However, that's the exception rather than the rule. Howard just dipped into his savings. He recently has connected with Mike Nelson at Red Rock Energy for a couple of investments that will help in the future. Duane is in some of the same investments, plus his real estate business and holdings. God has blessed them both. For example, Duane recently listed and sold a $1.7M golf course! They are both aggressive about missions, aggressive about prosperity, and they naturally enjoy converting wealth into ministry.

Networking the Church—Since Duane's India trip in April, much has been done through his local church. Desert Rock and a second local church have caught the vision, adopted a sister church attitude, and sent substantial monthly support for the pastors and orphanage. The church has a program for people to adopt orphans and tribal pastors that goes beyond our local congregation. Some of the things that have been accomplished are as follows: rebuilt a burned-out village, providing food and staples for the families until they could get back on their feet; expanded the orphanage and its influence; provided funds to expand two church buildings to accommodate growth from the crusades; provided for sending Pastor Anil's brother to another country to take a good paying engineer's position (he is sending monthly support back to India); feed the poorest pastors monthly; purchased a motorcycle for Pastor Anil; and provided for several outreach events. This effort has involved sacrifices by many through their love offerings. Duane initiated it by simply offering the opportunity for involvement to his pastor and the church.

The next trip—As I (Duane) think about this past year, the new-found relationships we have gained are priceless. I don't know of any better inheritance than this. I have other contacts in India who appear to be good candidates for working partners, and I'm making the time and finances to follow up with them. There is plenty of opportunity to get involved. The door in the Philippines is certainly open to anyone who will go and serve them well. Many of the pastors who attended the conference would be delighted to have teams from America expand their ministry impact. Bonifar has Bible students in training, ready and eagerly waiting their opportunity to pastor a village. This is obviously a very small sample of the opportunity for those who will respond to the need. Pray that the Lord will send forth workers into the harvest. The fields are ripe.

The next level is teaching disciples to fish. We're not only going to do crusades to help people find salvation and pastors' conferences to help them start churches, we're also going to teach them to multiply finances by starting businesses and engaging in commerce. We're going to teach Christians to be spiritual entrepreneurs (Kings). And, we're going to change the spiritual climate, the culture, and the economy.

Conferences and crusades in the third world are not the only expression of Kingly ministry. I know of two Kings who felt drawn to revitalize small towns in the Midwest . . . that's after blessing their own communities. Others are starting businesses or helping with micro-business loans, both locally and abroad. Bottom line— "spiritual" and "entrepreneurial" always have gone together.

CHAPTER 37
WRITE YOUR OWN TICKET

If I could add the most important ingredient that would help God's people become Kings, it would be "initiative." We theologically underestimate the role God wants us to play in implementing our hearts' desires and deciding what voluntary roles we could present to Jesus as gifts to help build the Kingdom and "do what the Father is doing." While millions of servants are asking the Lord, "What do you want me to do?" the Lord is looking for friends who will see and share His heart and lovingly *propose* "what they would like to do." As Solomon, the Lord is asking us, "What would you have me do for you?"

> *At Gibeon the* LORD *appeared to Solomon during the night in a dream, and God said, "**Ask for whatever you want me to give you**."*
> (I Kings 3:5) [Emp. added]

In addition to having goals, Kings need a personal business/ministry plan to really capture what they want to volunteer. Business plans usually describe a new start and are intended to convey the business concept and "sell" others on the idea—a loan officer for example. In this case, we first need to get our vision in writing and in enough detail to "sell ourselves" and gain the confidence to get started and finish.

Here's your assignment. The following outline is somewhat standard for a simple business plan. Prayerfully write your own "dream" and work your way through the details until it becomes real enough that you start to believe. Others can review and help . . . when it's ripe, they will resonate and confirm the reality of what you embrace by faith. Why the exercise? Something strange happens when you write out the details of the dream. It's a big step toward taking something that only exists by faith in the spirit realm and getting it to materialize in the real world.

Summary—Business/ministry concept, current situation, key success factors, financial situation/needs. Write this last. Assume some people will only read one page. So, on one page summarize the following sections.

Vision—What's the purpose and product of your endeavor. Why is it unique, compelling, valuable, and needed? Who will be attracted to it?

Marketing Plan—Who will be interested in your product or service? How will you let them know what you have? What is the value or price you will ask? What's the total demand? Who are your competitors? Why will you prevail in an open market? How is the industry changing? Will your competitive advantages remain in the future? What are the threats to and risks of this venture? How will you respond to them?

Products/services—Describe your product or service. Is there test-market experience? How will you make it available and distribute it? What is the potential to expand or provide additional products or services? How can your business or influence multiply?

Marketing and sales—How will you promote or market your product. What is your sales strategy or advertising scheme?

Operations—Who will manage the work and make the decisions? What are their qualifications? Who are the key personnel? What work will they do? How will you motivate them to share your dream and work with you? How will you train and compensate them? What facilities, services, and infrastructure will be required?

Financial Plan—What is your current financial condition? How will your family and business be supported? Will you need a loan? How will you transition from your current job or circumstance through the start-up phase?

Include two items:

➢ Personal financial statement—simply a one-page summary of all your assets and liabilities, summarizing your financial net worth at the bottom. You can get a free template for a financial statement at www.score.org/template_gallery.html.

➢ Cash flow statement—estimate all the monthly income and expenses related to your business or personal expenses for at least 12 months (or through your start-up phase, if longer). You can get an example format for a cash flow statement at www.score.org/downloads/C_12_month_cash_flow_statement.xls

Note: Consider making a financial plan from your personal budget and spending a few hundred dollars to get the accountant who does your taxes to formalize them for you. Treat your life and finances as a business—it really is the talent that God gave you and expects you to multiply.

KEY VI
I HAVE A MISSION—BLESS THE NATIONS
EXERCISES AND QUESTIONS

Peter Daniels of Adelaide, Australia has a 10 year mission. To raise up 100 multi-millionaires to do God exploits around the world. As one who has conquered dyslexia, negative affirmation (a modern day Jabez), Mr. Daniels has clear vision of what God wants him to do. It will take at least 10 years. He's 73. What a way to live as a King!!!!

1. What world changing goal will keep you passionate for the next 10 years?

2. What do you want on your tombstone? _____was a King, called to the marketplace by God. He accomplished_____
   _____.

3. What business initiatives will sustain your big dream?

4. What products and services need to be developed this year to prove to you and God that your words, heart, and actions are telling the truth?

5. Be like Joshua, "be very strong and courageous." DO IT!!!!!

KEY VII
I'M CONTAGIOUS—
VIRAL MISSIONS

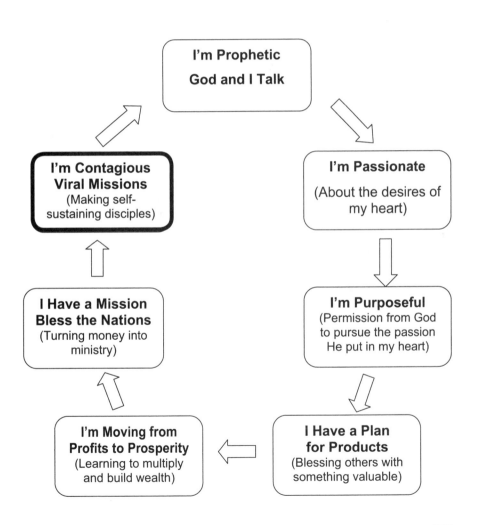

I'm Prophetic
God and I Talk

I'm Contagious
Viral Missions
(Making self-sustaining disciples)

I'm Passionate
(About the desires of my heart)

I Have a Mission
Bless the Nations
(Turning money into ministry)

I'm Purposeful
(Permission from God to pursue the passion He put in my heart)

I'm Moving from
Profits to Prosperity
(Learning to multiply and build wealth)

I Have a Plan
for Products
(Blessing others with something valuable)

E nthusiasm first appeared in English in 1603 with the meaning "possession by a god." The source of the word is the Greek *enthousiasmos,* which ultimately comes from the adjective *entheos,* "having the god within," formed from *en,* "in, within," and *theos,* "god." What do you look like with all seven keys present? You are motivated, contagious, catalytic, fervent, passionate, and fruitful to name a few. Here's where it leads.

The next reformation (sustaining revival)—The next revival will be in the marketplace and the revivalist is you. A grassroots movement of the saints, orchestrated by God Himself, is going to touch our cities and nations through the marketplace.

All by itself the soil produces—When all seven ingredients are present your life with start to flow. Circumstances, finances, and divine appointments will align themselves in your favor. You will "labor to enter into His rest." After that long taxi through the wilderness you finally take off and begin to soar. It's fun! Christianity spreads and sustains itself with a few of these catalysts present. We've called it revival or reformation in the past.

Viral Missions is not just an organizational initiative for large hierarchies to execute. It's a way of life that is built into the DNA of each of us. It's fun to heal the sick, raise the dead, cast out demons, and cleanse the lepers from a position of prosperity . . . really fun! Being entrepreneurial, finding prosperity and getting engaged in ministry isn't for the chosen few. It's for every believer. God is putting together a contagious, grassroots network that is being offered to every believer willing to admit he has been equipped for the work of ministry. It's always been in God's heart to have a personal interface with His people. That's a pretty flat organizational model with a viral ramp-up to the great commission.

CHAPTER 38
REFORMATION—SUSTAINING REVIVAL
IN THE MARKETPLACE

Fleeting revivals—The Church historically has seen remarkable revivals that brought about new experiences, and new doctrines that have brought us into a closer relationship with the God of Scripture. I was saved in the charismatic renewal in the early 70s and visited Toronto during the outpouring of the 90s. Both were wonderful experiences that lasted several years before dissipating. The unmistakable presence of God and the activity of the Holy Spirit touching lives are historically and experientially undeniable. They obviously leave you wanting more.

So why do they evaporate? One of the reasons for "disappearing revival" is that we see them as a sovereign move or visitation by God instead of the creation of a habitation for God by His people. Our tradition for revival is that it should happen in the Church for Christians. It certainly does touch the Church but there is a limit to confining the expression to church services. For example, the outpouring in Toronto resulted in special services nearly every night of the week for about five years. People from all over the world flew to Canada to experience what God was doing. However, there was no real concept that it should be taken to the city of Toronto. A great deal of activity was undertaken to find the same expression in other church meetings. I know we saw it in our own congregation (and it was wonderful). However, we really didn't even try to get it into the marketplace. Our concept was that the marketplace should come to the Church and experience it.

Reformation—God's real goal is to extend His Kingdom throughout the earth. He's releasing a dynamic in the Body of

Christ that is powerful enough to make it happen. The secret weapon is God's people. The world is waiting to see Christians who have joined the desires of their hearts with the will of God in a package that translates to "abundant life." Let's contrast the last reformation (compliments of Martin Luther) with what is happening now.

1. **The Bible was given to the masses (instead of Mass in Latin).** Luther and the Protestant Reformers read the Bible and understood that personal salvation was by grace. Jesus was known as Savior and Lord and men were understood to be His servants (Romans 3:23). Repentance, justification by faith, and a personal relationship with God was the primary emphasis.

    The Kingly reformation of today is headquartered in John 10:10. We understand that Jesus is also the King of Kings, and we are more than conquerors seated at His right hand. "Life" and "abundant life" are now added to the foundation of justification by faith.

    > *I am come that they might have life, and that they might have it more abundantly.*
    >
    > (John 10:10 KJV)

2. **A theological shift**—Reformations are undergirded by a new revelation, or emphasis, in Scripture. The Reformers emphasized the solution of the cross for personal sin . . . the death and burial of Christ as atonement for our sin.

    The Kingly reformation of today adds an emphasis to the resurrection of Christ. Jesus is seen as the giver of life. Instead of seeing Him way up in heaven, we see ourselves with Him, conversing with Him, co-laboring with Him to expand the Kingdom. In addition to knowing personal salvation, we also know the Savior personally and co-labor with Him from the status of "friend."

    > *I no longer call you servants, because a servant does not know his master's business. Instead, I have called you friends, for everything that I learned from my Father I have made known to you.*
    >
    > (John 15:15)

3. The Priesthood of the believer—The Protestant Reformers gave us the revelation that individuals personally have direct access to God and that the priestly ministry was not a singular conduit for biblical salvation.

The Kingly Reformation of today gives us the revelation that individuals personally have access to "ministry," and that it is not the sole function of the priesthood. God is "ordaining" Kings for ministry in the marketplace. It is the jailbreak that will allow the release of the saints equipped for the "work of ministry." We can fulfill the great commission to make disciples of all nations—with all of the saints.

> *So the word of God spread. The number of disciples in Jerusalem increased rapidly, and a large number of priests became obedient to the faith.*
> (Acts 6:7)

> *But the word of God continued to increase and spread.* (Acts 12:24)

> *In this way the word of the Lord spread widely and grew in power.* (Acts 19:20)

Sustaining revival in the marketplace—Your personal adventure that connects your dream, vocation, and the will of God is part of a much bigger plan that God is implementing to sustain revival. Here are a few of the ingredients.

Grassroots—We still have great evangelists, large churches, and influential organizations to reach the world. However, the "new look" is the awakening of individuals who are expressing their Kingly quotient for making a difference. Kings are discovering their dreams can be manifested. The marketplace move is being fueled by the saints themselves. The internet is facilitating global networks of peer relationships that rapidly are replacing the traditional hierarchy in government and business. God Himself is going to be the Head of the Church.

> **Note:** Although it is a secular book that merely cites Christianity as one example, *The Starfish and the Spider,* by Ori Brafman and Rod Beckstrom, is "must reading" on this aspect of our future.

The marketplace—The second distinctive is seen in the marketplace. We're going beyond crusades and church planting to teaching disciples how to be entrepreneurial and how to change the economies of nations. Freedom, property rights, and national prosperity are the outgrowth of a people who know the Lord and of a nation with a spiritual foundation.

> **Note:** *God Is at Work* by Ken Eldred provides the clearest case for the integration of commerce and missions, past, present, and future.

Our cities—The recent emphasis on united prayer, city-wide rallies, spiritual mapping, and pastoral cooperation was the beginning of a move to reach our cities. The claims of success have been overstated in the US because it stopped short of really getting out of our churches and into our cities. The foundational intent of these efforts has been to precipitate a sovereign move of God. It hasn't worked to completion because Christians have stopped short of getting involved in the community; in businesses, public office, schools, unions, and outreaches. We have not yet embraced the goal of redeeming the culture in our cities. Our vision has been too small; our schedule hasn't been scripted beyond our expectations for a premature rapture.

Leverage to bless the nations—Can any one man or organization make a difference? The logical answer is "no." However, what we really are doing is leveraged by the activity of the Holy Spirit and a host of unseen angels. When we embrace the vision to bless the nations and really change the world and put our hand to the task, a powerful dynamic begins. The Father works with us and our labors, our wealth, and our influence are multiplied a thousand times. God is calling a people out of mediocrity to embrace a vision for the nations; to fill the whole earth with His glory. He's already decided not to do it by Himself; nor will He do it through a single man nor a selected few. He's waiting for His Bride to put on her Kingly royalty and assume her authority on earth.

> *And when they found them not, they drew Jason and certain brethren unto the rulers of the city, crying, **These that have turned the world upside down** are come hither also. . . .*
>
> (Acts 17:6 KJV) [Emp. added]

Changing the world is a big task. We have to learn how to sow seed and let the soil produce all by itself.

CHAPTER 39
ALL BY ITSELF
THE SOIL PRODUCES

What the Kingdom is really like? I've been fascinated to learn how the Kingdom grows "all by itself." It's much easier than we usually think. If we're really going to "change the world" we have to leverage our activities so we operate beyond our human strength.

> He also said, "This is what the kingdom of God is like. A man scatters seed on the ground. Night and day, whether he sleeps or gets up, the seed sprouts and grows, though he does not know how. **All by itself the soil produces grain**—first the stalk, then the head, then the full kernel in the head. As soon as the grain is ripe, he puts the sickle to it, because the harvest has come."
> (Mark 4:26–29)

Here's the goal. "Seed" can be sown spiritually and the crop is a mature disciple. The parable of the sower is an example. "Seed" also refers to money or literal crops in the natural. People that know how to multiply money and disciples have learned how to do it easily, "all by itself." Let's consider both:

Finances—People with wealth do work hard but their focus isn't on the sweat, it's on the smarts (the wisdom of Proverbs). Wealthy people have learned to let money work for them. Have you heard of "passive income"? It's the best kind; shows up night and day with no effort on your part except to set it up in the beginning. I want to suggest that is "spiritual wisdom" and it reflects an aspect of Kingdom reality—"night and day, whether he sleeps or gets up, the seed sprouts and grows." We don't set out every day to re-earn our salvation. We set it up once at the cross and then start doing what the

Father's doing. It's not work; it's a joy to "flow" with the leading of the Holy Spirit and our heart's desire.

Even the key to engineering principles is to leverage nature to extract something for free. We build a dam and make electricity from the water that gives us free energy from gravity. We plant crops that grow naturally from the sun and water. Every good idea grows the Kingdom in an automated, natural way. That "natural growth" is true in engineering, finances, and our spiritual relationship with the Lord. If you can grasp it your creativity and productivity will change dramatically.

Natural Examples—The creativity that spawns great inventions or business concepts finds "workable" ideas; "Why didn't I think of that" is our usual response to the obvious genius of a great idea. When we hear it we can see that it will work easily... "all by itself the soil produces." Here are few examples.

Hydroelectric power—We build a dam and get free electricity. There are many in the Northwest and our power is less expensive than other areas because of it. Nuclear power is similarly easy. Just put fuel rods together and heat is generated that will also produce electricity.

Wine country—Wine growers in our area have discovered that our part of Washington is at the same latitude as the wine country in France. Vineyards and wineries are springing up everywhere in the last 20 years. In other areas its very difficult to grow wine grapes. Here, its really easy.

Starbucks originated in Seattle, and they recently announced a plan for 40,000 new stores. I wouldn't have guessed a cup of coffee that cost $3.75 would be a big hit. However, it's a treat that nearly everyone can afford. It works!

Ranching—Cows are like employees. The rancher gets to ride his horse, live in beautiful country, and watch babies being born. Each cow faithfully has a calf every spring that grows during the summer (even while the rancher is sleeping) and sells in the fall. They just have to live someplace where grass grows so all those "employees" and their calves get plenty to eat. If you own a business with employees you're reproducing yourself and multiplying your effectiveness. You can be on vacation and your company will still be performing it's mission.

Making disciples—I want to suggest that making disciples is much easier than we've believed in the past. Our "good news" message to new believers is sprinkled with terms like surrender, die, repent, turn, submit, and obey. Although there are powerful truths in each of those terms they must be balanced by the resurrection portion of the gospel.

You see "sin" is what makes life difficult. Cain murdered Able and the consequence of his sin is a great example. His "work" didn't multiply. His life became hard.

> *Now you are under a curse and driven from the ground, which opened its mouth to receive your brother's blood from your hand.* **When you work the ground, it will no longer yield its crops for you.** *You will be a restless wanderer on the earth.*
> (Gen. 4:11-12) [Emp. added]

When we get saved a spiritual door is opened to enter the Kingdom and the concept of multiplication can work for us too. What if our message to new disciples is that the consequence of their salvation was freedom, healing, abundant life, creativity, wealth, and generosity? What if we taught them they could arrange their lives by faith to receive these things passively (by grace)?

Here's what would happen. Disciples would start making themselves. Missions would go "viral." It would happen day and night and we wouldn't even understand all the reasons why these new disciples decided to start multiplying themselves without a lot of effort on our part. We just need to learn how to scatter the right seed!

Sowing the Right Seed—"Seed" can be God's word or money. Seed can also be our lives. In a very real sense we are seeds sown by God into the marketplace to produce a harvest. So how do we get the seed of our example to be something others will want to emulate? Our life has to "multiply" through this planting process. The degree of favor on our lives is like a bill board to others. They can see blessing before we say a word. Our lives are enticing testimonies as well as our words.

> *I tell you the truth, unless a kernel of wheat falls to the ground and dies, it remains only a single seed. But if it dies,* **it produces many seeds.**
> (John 12:24) [Emp. added]

We usually read John 12:24 as a death sentence for our heart's desires . . . our very life. We usually hear it as an admonition to give up everything. We expect things to go wrong in our life and then we read this verse and conclude that God is also trying to destroy us!

Let's put a different spin on this verse. Jesus did die over the course of a few hours. Since then the Kingdom has been multiplying and He's been sitting at the right hand of the Father (having a great time). This verse really speaks to the set-up required to have abundant life. Our old ways of poverty and hard work may have to die before we can "produce many seeds" and learn to multiply finances and disciples. If my life isn't multiplying and I'm stuck, what has to "change / die" to reach abundant life and "rest" while I'm doing it?

> *For he that is entered into his rest, he also hath ceased from his own works, as God did from his.* **Let us labour therefore to enter into that rest,** *lest any man fall after the same example of unbelief.*
> (Hebrews 4:10-11 KJV) [Emp. added]

It looks like this—God is multiplying the finances of His people because we looked for passive income and found the creative ideas that led us to "sow" inventions, investments, business opportunities, and ministries that multiply. People are drawn toward us because of the blessing they see operating. It's not work; it's an adventure. Our focus is less on ourselves and more on helping others find abundance. We tell others, "this is what the Kingdom is like, we scatter seed; it grows day and night and we don't know exactly how it works. We just know the soil produces, and we harvest . . . and we know it's a lot of fun!"

The main ingredient—When we see others prosper under the favor of God it's very natural to ask, "Can something this good happen to me?" The answer is yes. Wealth and fruitfulness in blessing others are God's will for you. God has not singled out certain people to bless at the expense of the rest of us. They have just discovered a few simple keys that we need to discover too.

> **Note:** Making your life "flow" is a very Biblical principle. It's also the envy of the new age movement and every other counterfeit spirituality out there. You can find a 1,000 false ways to hook up with "cosmic awareness." They all lead to "self" instead of Jesus.

1. Do What the Father Is Doing—The greatest power in the universe you can take advantage of is simply to do what the Father is doing. There are subtle changes in seasons and different emphasis in different areas. If you can pick up on the movement of the Holy Spirit in "your" hour and location and ministry gifts and you'll be amazed at the number of divine appointments you'll run into. For me, it's marketplace ministry. I run into people all the time that resonate with the great move that's going on around the world. Once you find the theme of your calling and map it in with what the Holy Spirit is already doing, things start to come together and adversity won't stop you.

> *I tell you the truth, anyone who has faith in me will do what I have been doing. He will do even greater things than these, because I am going to the Father. And I will do whatever you ask in my name, so that the Son may bring glory to the Father. You may ask me for anything in my name, and I will do it.*
>
> (John 14:12–14—see John 5:19–21)

2. Ability to Produce Wealth—If you want to translate God's favor to ministry, you have to navigate the harsh reality that it costs money. Instead of grieving we need to celebrate. God is all about life and life more abundantly. He's not afraid to show us how to "produce" wealth. It won't fall out of heaven. You have to get creative and find the idea that will produce it; part of your spiritual maturity as a King.

> *He gave you manna to eat in the desert, something your fathers had never known, to humble and to test you so that in the end it might go well with you. You may say to yourself, "My power and the strength of my hands have produced this wealth for me." But remember the* LORD *your God, for* **it is he who gives you the ability to produce wealth,** *and so confirms his covenant, which he swore to your forefathers, as it is today.* (Deuteronomy 8:15–18) [Emp. added]

3. It's more blessed to give—It is fun to give. Of course, we have to have something before we start—learn to receive from the Lord first. In fact, when we make disciples we don't just give them ministry and money; we teach them to prosper so they too can minister spiritually and naturally. Paul didn't depend on or covet the wealth of others. He created wealth with a good idea (tents in his case) and taught his disciples to do the same. He used that wealth to pull others up to his level.

> *I have not coveted anyone's silver or gold or clothing. You yourselves know that these hands of mine have supplied my own needs and the needs of my companions. In everything I did, I showed you that by this kind of hard work we must help the weak, remembering the words the Lord Jesus himself said: It is more blessed to give than to receive.'* (Acts 20:32–35)

Part of the reason people gain the favor of God to produce wealth is because God blesses generosity. Helping others is really an investment in the Kingdom that pays a dividend—even in the natural. People that already have wealth seem to understand giving better than those in poverty.

> *He who is kind to the poor lends to the LORD, and he*
> *will reward him for what he has done.*
>
> (Proverbs 19:17)

I'm excited about coupling ministry, missions, and micro-business ideas around the world. Imagine the strategy; a crusade to reach the lost and break the strongholds; church planting to mature the disciples; micro-businesses to send them back into the marketplace to produce wealth and ministry of their own. Sound's viral doesn't it? We're working with Mark Charles to connect the ideas, the Kings, the finances, and the opportunities (see www.releasing-kings.com/Mark-Charles.html). We've listed 10 business ideas on his interview site. Our goal is 1000's of ideas and 1000's of working examples of how to implement them. We're breaking poverty at the level of the welfare mentality and inviting God's people to pursue their heart's desires right into an abundant life. You're invited too.

When your seven keys to marketplace ministry are in place you'll be excited and contagious. Salt the earth with a few more like you and the mission of the church will become viral; a self-sustaining, grass roots revival that will cover the earth.

CHAPTER 40
VIRAL MISSIONS

Ideas change the world—I recently learned a new term (Viral Marketing—defined below) at a business retreat which we recommend (www.ibiglobal.com). At a recent conference in Huntington, WV, I met Mark Charles and posted his interview at www.releasing-kings.com/Mark-Charles.html. Somewhere between reading *The Starfish and the Spider*, the IBI retreat, our conference, and talking to Mark about micro-business the Lord is stirring a new concept (new to me anyway). Actually, it's as old as Eph. 4:12. First, the definition of viral marketing:

> **Wikipedia**—Viral marketing and viral advertising refer to marketing techniques that use pre-existing social networks to produce increases in brand awareness, through self-replicating viral processes, analogous to the spread of pathological and computer viruses. It can often be word-of-mouth delivered and enhanced online; it can harness the network effect of the Internet and can be very useful in reaching a large number of people rapidly.

The concept (Viral Missions)—New revelation births new terminology to describe it and new initiatives to attain it. A network of relationships (the body of Christ) needs a "big idea," or vision that releases the saints for the work of the ministry. For AA the ideology is simple: "If you have a problem with alcohol, stop consulting the experts, and lets help each other and follow the simple twelve steps," which are the implication of the ideology. For Skype, the motto is: "Lets talk on the phone for free!" What's "Viral Missions"? It's making missions affordable and fun . . . make disciples that make money to make a difference. Just sending money has a tendency to produce a welfare mentality and robs people of their initiative and responsibility. Viral missions has a goal of producing disciples who learn to multiply finances the same way you have and sustain themselves and their own ministries.

Yes, but how? The first thing you learn in traditional missions is how to take an offering within a denominational or mission hierarchy. Missionaries call it itinerating—an annual tour back in the states to rebuild the necessary financial support. Pastors aren't really hot on ideas that divert the church budget away from the church bills. So . . . let's let the tithes and offerings stay in the church so that we can have a quality staff to really do a good job of equipping the saints. I'm voting with the pastors on this one.

> **Please Note**: We're not throwing rocks at the traditional method of supporting missionaries. It's a good thing. We're simply saying we're on to something that involves more people and is more efficient.

What if we equipped God's people with ways to make money so they could fund their own mission trips? Think anyone would be interested? I do. I think there is an ageless generation prepared by God that is totally receptive to entrepreneurial adventures that run our cup over enough to fund missions. God is giving Christians amazing open doors right now. It's a season of increase that will not end in seven years . . . or 70 or 700.

What if these saints with enough financial flexibility did the ministry as well. Heal the sick, raise the dead, cast out demons, preached the crusade, and taught the conference. What if we stopped pretending that only "full-time" ministers can do that stuff and got back to Acts chapter 8 where the saints did the stuff? What if word got out that it was fun and anybody could do it? Might go viral! What if "viral" is Biblical. What if Christians had so much fun getting blessed financially and converting money into ministry that it became contagious.

> . . . *all except the apostles were scattered throughout
> Judea and Samaria.* Acts 8:1–2

Those who had been scattered preached the word wherever they went. Philip went down to a city in Samaria and proclaimed the Christ there. When the crowds heard Philip and saw the miraculous signs he did, they all paid close attention to what he said. With shrieks, evil spirits came out of many, and many paralytics and cripples were healed. So there was great joy in that city.

(Acts 8:4–8)

What if part of the ministry these Kings took to the third world was about making disciples who can make money; self-sustaining missions. What if we took a micro-business start-up package on every missions trip . . . to break the spirit "and" the practice of poverty? What if Kings had thousands of business concepts to choose from; each with a business plan and a recipe that addressed the cash flow and the accountability? What if those new micro-businesses made money and financed more ministry by the "nationals" themselves. Starting to sound "viral" again?

Back to Mark—What if there were no "what ifs?" Mark's vision is so practical and doable it's making my spirit leap. Think we're short of ideas? We posted ten from Mark's interview (www.releasing-kings.com/Mark-Charles.html). The Lord also gave him a divine appointment with SIFE (Students In Free Enterprise); an organization in business colleges intended to define businesses via student projects . . . already in 40 nations around the world and active in 1,600 campuses at a university near you! Many of their projects target third world applications.

Here's the Key. Missions is not just an organizational initiative for large hierarchies to execute. It's a way of life that is built into the DNA of every disciple. I need to add the frosting; it's fun to heal the sick, raise the dead, cast out demons, and cleanse the lepers from a position of prosperity . . . really fun! Being entrepreneurial, finding prosperity, and engaging in ministry isn't for the chosen few. It's for every believer. God is putting together a contagious, grassroots network that is being offered to every believer willing to admit he has been equipped for the work of ministry. It's always been in God's heart to have a personal interface with His people. That's a pretty flat organizational model with a viral ramp-up to the great commission.

> *A young man ran and told Moses, "Eldad and Medad are prophesying in the camp." Joshua son of Nun, who had been Moses' aide since youth, spoke up and said, "Moses, my lord, stop them!" But Moses replied, "Are you jealous for my sake? I wish that all the LORD's people were prophets and that the LORD would put his Spirit on them!"*
>
> (Numbers 11:26–29)

KEY VII
I'M CONTAGIOUS
THOUGHT QUESTIONS AND EXERCISES

1. The Warren Buffet/Bill Gates Foundation is meant to leave a legacy to the world. How can you, with your talents and business initiatives, create something that has a life of its own?

2. "Viral Missions" makes missions affordable and fun. I just heard of a creative idea that could utilize the technology of U-Tube, and bring real time revivals and miracles to you in your hand-held device. This could mobilize marketplace ministry and missions over the internet, blackberry, or traditional media "as it happens" cost effectively for the ministries in the field and the consumer. Take your dream and vision, and put a "viral business idea spin" to it. How could this idea mobilize thousands for years to come?

3. Take your "Viral Missions" idea, and replace the traditional missions offering mindset with the self-funding business mindset. Build ministry into your financials, streams of income, and profit centres, and take your marketplace missions idea around the world!

4. Let's get apostolic! God is merging miraculous works with financial exploits. If Peter or Paul lived in 2007, what kind of businesses might they own? What King or Prime Minister would they impact with their businesses, and their miraculous signs and wonders? Since Peter and Paul aren't here, but you and God are, finish your story. As God releases you to live this adventure, share it with us at www.desiretodestiny.com!

APPENDIX A
RECOMMENDATIONS

My own convictions about marketplace ministry have come gradually over the last several years. Reading several of Harold's books has made a huge personal difference. I've listed the "must reads" available at www.WorldcastPublishing.com.

THE NATURE OF GOD:

Who Is God

Precious in His Sight

THE NATURE OF MAN:

Jesus Came out of The Tomb—So Can You

Escaping Dualism

ESCHATOLOGY—STUDY OF FUTURE EVENTS:

Bringing the Future into Focus

Victorious Eschatology

MARKETPLACE MINISTRY (BY HAROLD AND JOHN)

Releasing Kings for Ministry in the Marketplace

OTHER RESOURCES ON OUR WEBSITE (WWW.RELEASING-KINGS.COM)

- Weekly ezine with a marketplace ministry theme
- Interview with Kings that are making a difference
- A store with our latest teaching materials and helps
- Information on upcoming conferences

APPENDIX B
THE DESIRE TO DESTINY
MARKETPLACE MENTORING SYSTEM

We are developing our "Desire to Destiny Marketplace Mentoring System" available at www.desiretodestiny.com. Our mission is to develop services and products to catapult you to your destiny! It's not enough to grasp the vision. We all need friends and wisdom to help us realize our individual dreams.

Consider us both a friend and a continual resource. David Harris is helping us develop this piece of the puzzle. David has a passion for seeing individual's dreams crystallize into a masterpiece.

Mr. Harris brings over 20 years of broadcasting and media experience, having helped launch two Christian radio stations in Canada. He has also worked with an international performance business coach and will help us develop the mentoring and coaching systems. David also owns and operates an investing and seminar business and will utilize these in the development of our conferences and events.

Initial considerations include:

1. Marketplace Mentoring Tools . . . a weekly newsletter

2. Releasing kings/Desire to Destiny Sponsorship Package . . . a turnkey package with steps, templates, advertising to host your own local Releasing Kings Conference

3. Launch Your Own Marketplace Ministry . . . help in launching your own marketplace ministry

4. Investment Workshops . . . specific opportunities to fund your vision for business in the marketplace

5. Personal Mentoring Project . . . opportunities for personal discovery, encouragement, and consulting help in identifying and implementing your business dream.

6. The Lives of Kings . . . Interviews and writings capturing real Kings at work in North America.

7. Releasing Kings Internet Radio Station . . . Explore this opportunity to support our journey.

We invite you to bring your ideas, suggestions, and stories to us at www.desiretodestiny.com.